Silver Tongue

Silver Tongue

Secrets of Mr. Santa Barbara

∾

STEVEN CRANDELL

2007 · Quinn, Rose, Elliot & Ellery, Santa Barbara, California

Published by Quinn, Rose, Elliot & Ellery, Publishers
402 East Gutierrez Street
Santa Barbara, CA 93101

Book design & Production: Eric Larson, Studio E Books
Cover design: Karen Owens, klo.design, www.klodesign.com

10 9 8 7 6 5 4 3 2 1
11 10 09 08 07 06

ISBN-10: 0-9789358-0-2 (hardcover)
        0-9789358-1-0 (paperback)

ISBN-13: 978-0-9789358-0-1 (hardcover)
        978-0-9789358-1-8 (paperback)

For my children,
Isaac, Luke, Josette and Nathaniel

Angels can fly because
they take themselves lightly.

—*G.K. Chesterton*

ACKNOWLEDGMENTS

FIRST thanks must go to Larry for living a remarkable life and displaying faith, flexibility and considerable restraint in allowing me to tell his story my way.

A number of people contributed to *Silver Tongue* by writing anecdotes about Larry. Each has helped paint part of the portrait. They are (in alphabetical order): Marv Bauer, Kate Carter, Bill Cirone, Ada Conner, Michael Crandell, Andy and Gena Davis, Jennifer P. Deacon, Michael Douglas, Stan Hatch, Ben Hellwarth, Joe Howell, Maryellen Kelley, Layla Khashoggi, Marsha Marcoe, Sherri Miller, Rita Murdoch, Tom Parker, John Robinson, Sal Rodriguez, Bob Scott, Pat Steele, Anne Smith Towbes, Paul Vercammen, Dr. Albert D. Wheelon, and Chancellor Henry Yang.

Some of Larry's dearest friends offered anecdotes that, due to space, were not included in this book. Their absence here does not imply an absence from Larry's affections. I heartily thank them for their effort and support.

The *Santa Barbara News-Press* kindly gave permission to use photos from their archive in this book. Photographer Joanne A. Calitri also allowed me to use her work. To both, I say thank you very much.

In addition, I would like to thank Stacy Bloodworth, Fred Klein, Marie Profant, Jeff and Karin Shelton and Phyllis Clancy.

I offer my deep gratitude: to David Dennis, for the inspiration to write the book; to the Devereux Foundation, for the financial support to get the manuscript completed; to Eric Larson of Studio E Books for serving admirably as both copy editor and book designer; to Karen Owens for her inspired cover design; to Kathleen, my wife, for her love and partnership; and to Marcy, my mother, for having an editorial touch as unfailing as her love.

Finally, I offer my appreciation to Grandma Jane, who inspired Larry to believe that love could make all the difference.

Are you happy?

Are you fulfilled?

Larry is.

Do you enjoy your community?

Do you laugh every day numerous times?

Larry does.

Can you speak in a way that touches people's hearts and opens their wallets?

Can you turn strangers into friends in a matter of minutes?

Larry can.

Read on, and I'll tell you how he does it.

Silver Tongue

The Brad Pitt Stratagem

IMAGINE a table of middle-aged women engaged in a pleasant lunch at a Santa Barbara eatery. The *maitre d'* approaches and politely explains that he cannot accept their payment for the lunch. The women are surprised. They are perfectly willing to pay their bill. The *maitre d'* shrugs as if to say the matter is already settled; then he leans in as if letting them in on a secret.

Brad Pitt, he says in hushed tones, happened to be passing by the restaurant and admired them from afar. Mr. Pitt, however, was too shy to say hello. So he decided to pay for their meal as a token of his esteem.

There follows a delicious moment when the women consider the possibility that this could be true. Then the smiles start to bloom on their faces and the giggles bubble forth. The diners now suspect the truth. They crane their heads to look for Larry Crandell. After all, he had stopped by to say hello earlier. And they know his *modus operandi*. But when they scan the room for the man who would be Brad Pitt, he has already made his exit.

It's a scenario that has played out dozens of times all over town. From down-to-earth cafés to the ritziest of restaurants in Santa Barbara, Brad Pitt has been picking up checks for women at lunch, admiring them, but always too shy to show himself. And the objects of Brad's admiration? They all wear big smiles as they leave the restaurant, shaking their heads and chuckling.

Larry loves to eat out, but not for the food. He has a very basic palate—the blander, the better. He likes his meat well done and his salad (lettuce and tomato) without dressing. No booze, no coffee, no tea. Just Diet Coke—on ice, by the crate.

Larry could care less for *haute cuisine*. He goes to restaurants for the social interaction. He always sits facing the entrance so he can see who comes in. He loves to "work the room," as he calls it, saying hello to everyone he knows, making them feel at ease and telling a few jokes. But he also likes to set up the Brad Pitt Stratagem as he leaves. He enjoys the fact that when he exits the restaurant he leaves behind a time-bomb of merriment. He says all it costs is money, and the people who get treated by "Brad Pitt" get a happy experience which will last the rest of the day.

At the heart of the stratagem is Larry's essential philosophy. He does things for people that they enjoy *and he enjoys*. In this way he is both giver and receiver. There is no greater joy for him than feeling he has helped someone feel good or laugh or just enjoy life. In the moment when the women diners consider the possibility that Brad Pitt actually admired them, they feel excited. Larry feels excited, too. It's a circle of fun that fuels itself—which is why he keeps on doing it.

Of course, he doesn't always pretend to be Brad Pitt. Larry is nothing if not resourceful when it comes to generating variations on a theme.

A few years back, a prominent male philanthropist in town had his bill picked up by Meg Ryan. She, like Brad Pitt, was too shy to say hello in person. A week later, Larry received a card in the mail. It was from the philanthropist's fiancée. She suggested that though she understood why Meg might be attracted to her husband-to-be, she would "break Meg's legs" if she ever came near him.

Another time, Warren Buffett, the world's second richest man, picked up the bill for a table of millionaire businessmen in Montecito. Later, Larry heard from one of the high-powered investors, who told Larry he thought Jimmy Buffet might have been a more appropriate pseudonym given Larry's level of investment insight.

This kind of jocular insult is food and drink to Larry. It's male-speak for "I'm enjoying your company." As such, it was all the indication Larry needed to confirm that his Warren Buffett Stratagem had been a success.

Appreciating

THIS BOOK might make you think. It might make you smile. It might even lead you to think and smile at same time—perhaps about someone you love.

I am thinking and smiling about my father right now. Sometimes it seems we spend a lot of our lives thinking and frowning. My father has spent his life trying to get people to do the opposite. He seeks to unite thought and emotion in order to create pleasure. You have to admit, it's a delightful place to be as a person—using your brain and your heart together, and to positive effect.

So here's the second secret to be revealed in these pages. You see, my father found a shortcut to this idea of thinking and smiling at the same time. He calls it *appreciating*.

Here's a diagram:

Thinking & Smiling → *Appreciation* →
Shared Joy → *Affection & Love*

If you don't get it now, don't worry. Just read. This is like the boat rides at Disneyland my dad used to take me on in the 1960s. There are really tracks underneath the water, and no matter how much you steer like hell, you can't really crash. So relax.

Anyway, I'm the writer. And, as my dad is fond of saying, I work alone.

What Is This Book About, Anyway?

GOOD QUESTION. But remember, I work alone.

The book examines the talent of Santa Barbara's Silver Tongue. It looks at his four central abilities:

- to make people laugh
- to make them feel good (even as he insults them)
- to build unity (even as he plays the part of the verbal rebel)
- and, mostly, to motivate.

In short, this book is about the *power of words*.

Of course, as my father well knows, the power of words is anything but straightforward. Used by a skilled public speaker, words are often just a clever disguise. Larry will freely confess as much. It may come as a shock to the many people who have listened to him and laughed at his improvised, rascally humor, but his motives are far more serious than his repartee. Even his funny stories often have a secret mission. Confront him. Ask him flat out. He'll tell you. He uses the power of words to invoke the power of love.

Here are the main premises of Larry's philosophy.

- Every loving act carries with it the power to transform lives, so all kindness matters.

- Both the giver and the receiver benefit from compassion—sometimes in far-reaching and unexpected ways.

- Reaching out to show love is not only good for the spirit, it can be the key to one's destiny.

Here's an example of what I'm talking about.

Once upon a time, during the Depression, there was a woman

named Jane who raised and supported three sons on her own. They lived in Newark, in a particularly blighted part of the Garden State. Jane worked full-time as a shoe clerk. The family was on relief—as they called welfare in those days. The boys went to the YMCA to stay off the streets. Jane loved her sons, urging them to believe in themselves, to be generous and to appreciate what they had. Decades later, when her eldest moved with his family to the earthly paradise of Santa Barbara, California, he took his mother's philosophy with him. There, in one of the wealthiest areas of the United States, he succeeded spectacularly—not in making money, but in helping others give it to good causes.

He became a jovial and gentle Robin Hood, lightening the wallets of the rich—and leaving them all the happier for their donations. After more than four decades, his volunteering, his leadership and his wit are so widely known that the local newspapers call him Mr. Santa Barbara.

From a nobody in Newark to Mr. Santa Barbara—that's the power of love at work.

Larry Crandell is in his eighties, but you'll find him at work in his office six or seven days a week. He doesn't put his success down to hard work or luck or even his cheeky sense of humor. For him, it's all about love. For him, the definition of love begins and ends with his mother's appreciation of, and devotion to, him and his brothers. Jane would sometimes say to Larry in all seriousness, "Cast your bread upon the waters, and it will come back toasted."

Larry knew that she was really talking about love, the faith it engenders and the remarkable things it can achieve.

The Chain Reaction of Love

GRANDMA JANE'S love inspired my father to a career helping others. One of the people he helped was me—his fourth child of five, his third son.

My father's love brought me home again.

I'm 47, with four kids, two marriages, one divorce and a graying goatee. I was living in New Zealand one day in 2005, minding my own sleep-deprived existence, pulling a 4:30 A.M. to 12:30 P.M. shift producing the national news for Television New Zealand. Then my dad called. He wanted to start a business with me. He was willing to guarantee me a salary while we got started. He said he was "confident without being certain"—one of his favorite phrases—that we could start a consultancy advising nonprofit organizations on fund-raising.

A few months later, I arrived in Santa Barbara, wife and children at my side. I had been away for 15 years. Now I was back in a gorgeous place, with most of my immediate family and all of my extended family. It was thrilling. My heart resonated with my homecoming, and I felt a deep gratitude to my father for having the audacity to bring me home.

Here's the denouement of this little story. After my father and I had already decided I would move to Santa Barbara, David Dennis, then the executive director of the Devereux Foundation here, approached my father. Devereux is a national organization which cares for people with developmental, emotional and educational disabilities. It was a big-hearted charity already. But though it had been operating in Santa Barbara for 60 years, few people had a good idea of what it really did. David wanted to reach out to the community, so he asked my father if Devereux Santa Barbara could be the Crandell Company's first client. One of our first tasks, he said, would be to produce a book about Larry's life. To seal the deal, he asked my father how much we needed to make ends meet, and then agreed to pay it.

Of course, Devereux was one of the charities Larry had helped in the past 40 years. Now they were helping us so that we could help them.

The power of love. I write these words knowing they would not be here on this page if not for my father's love or my grandmother's or even the love David Dennis felt for Devereux which led him to find a creative solution that suited everyone.

One Good Shot Deserves Another

Interspersed throughout this book, you will find what I call "Silver Tongue Stories." These are eye- (and ear-) witness accounts of Larry in action, gathered with the generous help of people who know him. The idea is to give you an added dimension of insight to Larry by letting his friends, family and acquaintances speak directly about him. Whenever you see this heading, you'll know that what follows is testimony from someone who experienced the inimitable effects of the Silver Tongue.

The first of these stories is from Michael Crandell, Larry's second son and former business partner.

∾

WHEN we had an office on De La Vina Street, Larry was driving an old army green Cadillac acquired from his doctor and basketball buddy, Dr. Tony Allina. The car was "hu-nor-mous." Next door were two lawyers specializing in bankruptcy. One day one of them walked into the office and asked for Larry.

"I'm terribly sorry," the lawyer said to Larry. "I've bumped into your car in the parking lot and caused some damage."

Larry paused and looked at him seriously.

The lawyer continued, "Of course I'll pay for it, get you a rental in the meantime—whatever you want." The poor man was clearly embarrassed. "Please," he said, "Let me know what would make up for it."

Larry paused another moment. "What kind of car do you drive?" he asked.

"A BMW," said the lawyer.

"Okay," said Larry, "Just let me have one good shot at your car, and we'll call it even."

—*Michael Crandell*

Always Mix Business with Pleasure

TWO or three years ago, one of Larry's admirers sent him a birthday note with a quote from the French literary pioneer François René de Chateaubriand. Larry has since copied it out longhand and keeps it in his wallet. He is fond of producing the well-creased note paper at meetings and reading from it. The quote captures, he says, what he has tried to do with his life. This is how it goes:

> *A master in the art of living draws no sharp distinction between his work and his play. His labor and his leisure. His mind and his body. His education and his recreation.*
>
> *He hardly knows which is which. He pursues his vision of excellence through whatever he's doing and leaves to others to determine whether he is working or playing. To himself he always appears to be doing both.*
>
> *—François René de Chateaubriand*

People marvel at Larry's longevity, his productivity, his resilient health, his buoyant spirit. The secret lies in his approach to giving— he does it as much to have fun as to do good. It's that simple. When work and play are the same thing, good fun becomes fun good.

(By the way, Larry says the quote impressed him in one other way. He now knows a literary giant can be named after a steak.)

Plumbing Love

MY FATHER likes to say that no one has yet plumbed the depths of his capacity to accept praise. I take his word for it. No one knows the plumbing like the person who lives there.

He also says he loves shallow things deeply (Oscar Wilde), and that he's rich in the fewness of his wants (Socrates). You get the idea. Clever guy. Sense of humor. Not disconcerted by irony—actually revels in it. Like any silver tongue, my father is often seduced by an apt thought dressed in a felicitous phrase.

"Self-praise hath a great stench," Larry will say, quoting Samuel Johnson. Praise from others, however, is always welcome. In fact, if praise were a doughnut, Larry would eat it in two bites. But in being honest about his hunger for positive feedback, and in making fun of his own egocentric focus, he comes across as refreshingly frank. His humor often strikes a strange and graceful balance—being concurrently self-centered and self-deprecating.

He meets a woman at a breakfast for a nonprofit. Linen and silver are on the table. Hundreds of powerful business people chat in one of the classiest hotels in town. Larry has a big, welcoming smile. "I just wanted to tell you," he says, leaning in close, "how happy you are to meet me."

Laughter ensues. Larry has turned a mundane moment into merriment. The woman later tells Larry how funny he is. It's another test of his capacity to accept praise. And once again, he finds a way to make room. His depths remain unplumbed.

This book is not a biography of Larry—I don't have the objectivity for that task. But neither is it an attempt to turn him into a saint. I come not to praise Larry, but to understand him. And the first step in that process is appreciating the role love plays in his life.

* * *

My father tells stories that are ripe with allusions and digressions—so ripe you could say they are fruitful and multiply in direct relation to the proximity of the punch-line. Everything reminds him of something. Anyone who has listened to him can attest to the fact that his story tributaries flow together to form a stream-of-consciousness resembling a verbal Mississippi. (Larry calls it creating a "mood.") But despite his sponge-like approach to praise and his fascination with the sound of his own voice, there is something profoundly other-oriented about Larry. Service to the community. Service to others. Not because it's a duty. Because he feels inspired to help. Because compassion spurs him to action. Because he enjoys it. For all his verbal tap-dancing and his fondness for the emotional shallows, he really is a deep guy. Love makes him so. It is the motivation that makes the flatlands of anyone's spirit into mountains and valleys, rainforests and deserts. My father loves praise, but he loves love more.

Love is the ultimate paradox. It brings pleasure and disappointment, meaning and despair. Love is a package you've been expecting that finally arrives only for you to find that it's not exactly what you ordered. The trick, for me, is in appreciating what's inside—no matter the shape, size or apparent usefulness.

Acceptance and appreciation. My father is brilliant at both—but his definition of love also includes compassion.

I remember sitting in a café with him. He pointed and whispered, "Turn around." I saw a middle-aged woman, overweight, in polyester pants and a t-shirt. What struck me first was that most people would be embarrassed to eat their Sunday morning breakfast cereal in that outfit, much less go out to a café in it. But I didn't notice what my dad did. He whispered again, "Look at her feet." Then I saw. One running shoe sheathed a flesh-and-bone foot. The other shoe was on a prosthesis with a steel post running up the pants leg. My father shuddered as if his own foot had just been amputated. "We don't know what we have," he said.

My father has spent the latter part of his life acting on that compassion. He does it by helping local nonprofit organizations. He's volunteered his leadership for hundreds and hundreds of fund-raisers over four decades. By creating new ways to raise money in the Santa Barbara community, he's brightened the financial prospects of many nonprofits. As an emcee and an auctioneer, he's injected humor into the awkward task of asking for money. Yes, he enjoys the limelight. Yes, he excels at the mike. Yes, he's a glutton for recognition. But his chief joy can be summed up in one word—people. And people need love.

Grandma Jane

I have a confession to make. I don't know how I'm going to end this book. And yes, I know the cardinal rule of writing and bus driving: If you don't know your destination, you may have trouble reaching it. But I can tell you this much: I'm not sweating this one. There are only two destinations in life. Love and loss. My story, my dad's story, and everyone else's if they care to think about it, is heading in the same two directions. At the same time.

Love and loss. Grandma Jane knew all about them.

I wrote the following for the extended family at Christmas 2004. The piece is based on tape-recorded comments my father made about his childhood. Using a little poetic license and a lot of love, I tried to write from Larry's point of view. I tried to write the story of what it was like to be Jane's son. Here it is.

∾

THIS IS a story about my mother. She's dead now. She died more than forty years ago. But she lives inside me still. That's the way love works. Some things are stronger than death.

Her name was Jane. Her life was devoted to her children, myself and my two younger brothers, Sam and Marty. She worked hard. She never complained. She enjoyed giving.

The story of Christmas is the story of a love that is never extinguished. My mother had that kind of love—indestructible, unconditional, always forgiving, never in doubt. Jane had her faults. But her love was the rock of my life. She was the architect of me.

I was born April 5, 1923, in Lynn, Massachusetts, a suburb of Boston. But Newark, New Jersey, was where I grew up. Almost all my memories of childhood come from there. We moved to Newark in 1930 because my father's company failed. He was in the shoe business—either a manufacturer's representative or a partner in a shoe manufacturing firm, I'm not sure. It was during the Great Depression. Lots of people unemployed, lots of people on relief. Our family was on relief, too.

But at least my mother had a job. She worked at a department store called Hahnes. She sold shoes. She worked full-time. In those days, it meant nine to five, six days a week. And all for 19 bucks. It wasn't enough to pay the rent at Broad Street, so we moved to Oriental Street. Picturesque name, but there was nothing fancy about it. We had a one-bedroom apartment over a bar and grill. Five hundred square feet, three children under 10. My two brothers and I slept on the daybed in the living room. And I slept very soundly through the breaking of bottles and the drunken singing and the arguments from the bar downstairs because I suppose I didn't know very differently. Kitchen aromas drifted up to our apartment from the grill. Some of them were less than appetizing. I think it was there that I developed my sensitive nose for food smells.

There was a barber across the street. His name was Ace. He used to work on his hand and arm strength by pulling and squeezing a piece of rubber. He charged us 25 cents a haircut. Because we were poor. Normal price was 75 cents. But life in the 1930s, when you knew no other one, wasn't particularly harsh or difficult. Of course, it was pretelevision. When you went to the movies on Saturday, as a kid, it cost ten cents. You got two full-length features, plus a comedy, plus a newsreel, plus a serial. We would go to the movies at 12:30 in the afternoon and get out at 5:00. Four and a half hours of entertainment. All for 10 cents. We didn't have a car from the time I was five. So I didn't really miss it. If we wanted to go somewhere, we took the bus. Or walked.

In the part of Newark where we lived, there were no parks and no trees. After I was about 10 years old, there was no father around either. My dad was born in 1875. He was at least 16 years older than my mother. He was 47 when I was born. My mother was head of the house. My dad was sick. He suffered from alcoholism and maybe some other things. My mother said he had muscular atrophy of the spine, but I don't recall his being physically infirm. My mother used to go to sleep with a towel wrapped around his arm and her arm because sometimes he'd slip out and wander the streets of Newark. On several occasions my mother sent me to look for him. I was eight or nine years old. I usually found him, and I don't have any recollection of that being an unpleasant thing. I'd say, "Hey, Dad, it's time to go home." And it worked out. I remember him giving me a dollar and telling me it was his last and sending me out to get Bromo-Seltzer. I remember flipping the bottle up and catching it as I walked. I remember the thrill of the risk I felt as I considered the possibility that I might drop it, that I might have to tell my father I'd wasted his last dollar. I don't remember ever being punished physically, but I had the feeling that if I displeased him I would be punished verbally. He just stayed in bed a lot during the day. He was short with his answers. He was cranky and unpleasant. And perhaps for good physical reasons, he felt defeated. In any case, I didn't feel any love. But my mother did a great job of building him up. She added as much of a positive nature as she could to my father's exploits. She created a legacy of accomplishment and pride and honor. One of her embroidered tales was that my father had been a lieutenant in the Rough Riders with Teddy Roosevelt in the Spanish American War of 1898. I think we later found out he was a drummer boy.

My mother didn't go to work as a shoe clerk until the early 1930s. That's when my dad was admitted to the Veterans Hospital in Summit, New Jersey—20 miles from Newark. Without an automobile, 20 miles was a long distance. And here is where one of my mother's most startling accomplishments comes in. During a period of 20 years, she didn't fail even once in her weekly visits to my father. It required two lengthy bus rides and dropping us off to stay with relatives. But she always did it. It was usually a Sunday. She brought my dad things to eat or little presents. When I got to be 14 or 15, she started taking me along. When we arrived, he seemed to blame her for everything, as people sometimes do when things aren't going well. They blame whomever's handy. He'd say the food's terrible. You're 15 minutes late. And so on. And after two or three visits, she and I agreed that I should stop going. I loved my mother very much. She was a very, very gentle person. And I resented his tone. But after that I didn't see him much. Did I tell you? He had the same name as me. Lawrence Leith Crandell.

Nineteen dollars a week was a very minimal wage. So we had to do what a lot of people did during the Depression, shop at stores that charged more but offered credit. One day I went to Angelo's, a butcher and grocer who gave us credit, and I charged three oranges for ten cents. When I brought them back to my mother, she cried. She cried because even ten cents spent on something unplanned threw the budget out of kilter. But don't feel sorry for me. We were very poor, but I didn't feel poor. I felt the opposite. My mother made a big thing of the four of us together. The three boys and her. And she succeeded so well that I felt sorry for kids who lived in houses with yards, kids who didn't rely on relief to eat lunch, kids with clothes that fit, kids who had fathers around. You see, they didn't have what we had. They weren't part of our family. My mother convinced us that we were a great family. And we enjoyed our lives. At camp or the Y, when one of the brothers was competing at sport, we were proud. We'd announce to everyone in earshot: "That's my brother!" When we visited Mom where she worked, she would always drop everything to introduce us to her clients and co-workers. She was proud of us. We felt it down in our bones. We believed we were lucky, and so we were. And Mom, she just kept the appreciation coming. She even spoke beautifully about my dad. And whenever my mother had a free day, we'd have an outing. We'd take a bus ride around the whole town. It would take a couple of hours. A big circle route, ending where we started. It cost five cents for everyone because they didn't charge for children. So we would do that. We'd just sit there and look out the window and ride the bus. And we liked it. It was a fun thing. Our family activity.

Once, while we were on one of those bus outings, my mother got up and sat next to a stranger and said, "Those are my children." The man recoiled and looked away. But Jane persisted. "Don't you think they're wonderful?" she said. "Yeah, very nice," he answered. Then she came back and sat next to us and said, "You know, that man couldn't stop raving about you." She was determined to give us the feeling that we were loved and admired. And we enjoyed it—even though we knew that as a reporter of events, my mother lacked not only objectivity, but also credibility.

My mother left school after the third grade, but she revered education. She expected us to do well. My school was Webster Street School. Fifty percent African American, 50 percent second generation Italian-American. No one believed my last name was Crandell. I wasn't black, so I must be Italian. The teacher asked me if I was sure my name wasn't Crandelli. I came to Newark with this Bostonian accent. "Oh, look at the brah-nch." " I'm going to take a bah-th." When they heard that at the Webster Street playground it was a signal to pound on me. Two or three guys would corner me and say, "Lawrence, you talk like a sissy." Then they'd punch me. They wouldn't hit me in the face, just punch me in the arms.

My mother felt that knickerbockers with an elastic waist were the proper attire. They wore knickerbockers all over America, but not in Webster Street School. And so I was the subject of ridicule. and the other kids would come up behind me and pull my pants down. I responded immediately to the abuse by pleading for my life. I had about five fights and lost them all. But the balance of power switched in the classroom. I'd say, "Charlie, they're going to ask you when was the War of 1812." He'd say, "Oh yeah, what's the answer?" As I look back, I don't think there was a tremendous amount of ill will. They'd say, "We'll get you in the playground, Lawrence." I'd say, "Yeah, if you're smart enough to find the playground."

When I was in the eighth grade, the teacher said that for the first time in her teaching career she had two students out of 30 who were capable of doing high school work. The teacher was referring to a girl named Edith and me. And she said, "I'm not sure about this, but it's possible that Lawrence even has the ability to go on to college."

She was right. I did go to college. So did my brothers. Later I wrote a story at Syracuse. I got an A-minus. The teacher said I should send it to a publisher. It was about my mother. It said that when my brother Sam was Phi Beta Kappa and got his master's degree from the University of Chicago, it was my mother up at the podium receiving the sheepskin. When my brother Marty stood over a fallen foe in the ring, it was my mother who got the Golden Gloves as the national in-ter-collegiate heavyweight boxing champion. When I scored a basket, she was there.

She was also there for me when I least expected it.

I had just finished high school, and my mother wanted to give me a present. So she got 600 bucks from someplace, which was a huge amount for her—two-thirds of a year's income. Then she bought me a 1939 Plymouth—it had the stick shift on the steering wheel. Only a couple of years old. I felt very suave. I also felt she was doing some-thing unwise. But she wouldn't hear a word of it. One of Jane's sayings was, "Don't tell me I'm being generous. I'm enjoying this more than if I were getting something." And she did enjoy giving me the Plymouth. Almost as much as I enjoyed driving it around.

But one of my favorite memories of my mother came when all three of us brothers were young. She would walk us to the Eighth Avenue Day Nursery—a child care place—subsidized by the Community Chest, now known as the United Way. We loved walking with our mother. But the walk itself presented a problem. You see, we had to take turns holding her hand. She would say, with great pleasure, "I have three sons, but I only have two hands." That was typical of her. Whatever amount of corn you see in me, it's honestly come by. We would count the blocks in each direction, about a mile and a half each way. Marty got to hold her hand all the time because he really needed to—he was only about three—and Sam and I alternated.

We didn't have to hold her hand, we wanted to. It was a privilege and a pleasure. One that I will never forget. As I will never forget her. My mother. Jane Rosenthal Crandell.

A Jog-a-thon with a Surprise Ending

ALTHOUGH I have never seen her, in my mind's eye she wore sensible shoes, a blue gingham dress and had the face of Larry Crandell—when he was 70. No, I'm not referring to Larry in drag at a celebrity waiters fund-raising luncheon. I'm referring to Larry's beloved mother, Jane, whom he remembers wistfully as a "handsome" woman. For all intents and purposes, Grandma Jane was a single mother. She raised her three sons on limited resources, but managed to provide them with an abundance of love. She struggled more than she should have, and it was noticed by her son.

Over time Larry has found many ways to support our community publicly by shaking the hands of the rich and famous for good causes, but there are just as many quiet gestures that Larry has made to ease life's little struggles. I would venture that Larry has spent a surprisingly large amount sponsoring the under-12 set in school jog-a-thons, gift-wrap sales, Girl Scout cookie sales, raffles, bake sales, candy bar sales and magazine subscription drives. With at least some of this financial support, he has eased the burden of a single mom or dad who was struggling—perhaps a bit more than they should.

In 1999, my then seven-year-old son strutted through the front door of our home holding aloft a trophy for the most money raised in the school jog-a-thon. These funds would help me pay for his passage on a much-anticipated sixth grade trip. "How many people sponsored you?" I asked him in surprise. Eyes squinting with delight, his broad gap-tooth grin gave way to an explosion of laughter. "Just one!" he said. "I asked Mr. Crandell to sponsor me and he said he would give me twenty dollars." I tried to explain that it was probably Larry's intention to make a flat $20 contribution, but my son insisted.

Later, I called Larry to explain the misunderstanding, letting him know we had no expectation of more than $20. Larry, who at the time was jogging regularly at the SBCC track, graciously stood by his commitment to the $20-per-lap pledge. Then he asked, "So how many laps did the little guy run in an hour?"

I explained that my son had run 38 laps around the schoolyard. There was a pause. I could sense Larry calculating his commitment. "Well," he said, "you've got quite a little athlete on your hands! I'll put the check in the mail."

—*Jennifer P. Deacon*
Assistant dean, development,
Donald Bren School of Environmental Science & Management,
University of California at Santa Barbara

You Don't Find Your Passion, It Finds You

Larry's first public speech was delivered in 1935, in the middle of the Great Depression. He was 12 years old. Although he describes himself then as a "smart-ass," he was sorely lacking in confidence and a sense of self-worth.

Despite this, his first time at the microphone, believe it or not, was at a fund-raiser. For the YMCA.

This little fact means Larry has been at the microphone on behalf of charity for more than 70 years. No wonder he seems so comfortable there. No wonder he can ad lib so naturally.

It was not always so. Larry says this first speech was at once terrible and intoxicating. Here's how he recounts the story.

∽

I WAS not very good at sports. Somehow, no matter the game, I was always the last one chosen for pickup games in the schoolyard. When I did play, no one would throw me the football. You see, I didn't have a father around to teach me all the subtleties of sports and life. It took the YMCA to open up sports for me.

Our Y was in the heart of downtown Newark, so we had to take a bus to get to it. My brothers and I spent all day there every Saturday. (My mother had to work Saturdays.) We became proficient at ping-pong because we played it literally for hours on end. The Y was baby-sitting us, basically. It was pretty widely known that we were charity cases.

One day the executive director asked me if I would go to a YMCA membership meeting and talk about summer camp and what the Y meant to me. I said yes, but I felt uncertain and anxious.

It was during my homely period—which so far has only lasted about eight decades.

I remember getting up on the day of the speech and looking in the mirror and seeing these piggy eyes and pimply face. There wasn't a muscle in my entire body. My confidence was at a low ebb. I just hadn't had the little victories that some people get at T-ball or YFL or that sort of thing.

I remember being introduced that fateful evening as "Lawrence Crandell," and I stood and confronted my first audience. I don't recall the exact size of the crowd, but there were lots and lots of people there.

I don't remember what I said, but I remember the way I said it. I got red in the face and I sputtered and talked about my mother. I talked about Camp Kiamesha, 60 miles away, where we swam in the lake and enjoyed the out-of-doors. I spoke about the YMCA as our main place to play sports. Ping-pong, basketball, swimming. But I did not speak well. In fact, I mostly remember my halting delivery—more stops and starts than a milk truck. And no jokes. No engaging stories. Just a tall, awkward and probably boring 12-year-old.

However, the most important part of this story wasn't my subject or how I spoke. The most important part is that at the end of the speech people applauded.

People actually applauded.

I was surprised. And relieved. It hadn't occurred to me that anything I did in life would gain applause. It felt good—like appreciation and approval all rolled into one.

Someone has characterized applause as the "sweetest sound in the world." It certainly was on that day in 1935. Today it still is. And here I am still jumping up on my hind legs seeking it.

You know, that was 71 years ago. I think I was mostly relieved to have the speech over with at the time. Since then I've learned how to gauge an audience, how to connect with them, how to tell a story. Since then I've come to experience a feeling of exultation when speaking—as if this was what I was meant to do in life. When I was 12, I was just astonished that they cared enough to clap for me.

That was my start, only I didn't know it then. Even though I served as a bombardier in World War II, I've gone through life as a tail-gunner—always seeing where I've been and not having much of a clue about what is coming.

I think that's okay. We don't always need a plan. Some of us have never had much of one. To quote Shakespeare, as my wife, Marcy, is wont to do, "The readiness is all."

Larry Crandell or Michael Douglas?

IN THE 1990s, my family and I joined with many people in Santa Barbara to help create the 70-acre Douglas Family Preserve in Santa Barbara—a beautiful area on the coast with public access. The Parks and Recreation Community Foundation (PARC), which helps look after the preserve, held an annual event at which it gave its Philanthropist of the Year award. I attended four years in a row to help raise money for the preserve.

One year Larry came up to me and said, "Michael, I've got to get you in the act, because even though I'm more talented, people came to see you." Here's this guy in his seventies running around with the energy of a 30-year-old. "Is it okay if I clown around?" he said. How could I say no?

A few minutes later, he got me up on stage before a crowd of several hundred people, most of whom were middle-aged. "This morning our star here," he said, indicating me, "spoke to 925 nubile co-eds at UCSB." I'm a graduate of UCSB and had given a speech there earlier that day. "These young students cheered and fussed over him," Larry continued, "but you women here, I want to talk to you. You're more sophisticated. You understand what makes a man really attractive. So I'm going to ask you to vote: who do you think is more attractive— Larry Crandell or Michael Douglas?"

There was a moment of stunned silence. But Larry didn't miss a beat. He held his hand over his own head and asked for applause. There was a strong round of clapping. So I said, "Do me." Another strong round of applause. I said, "It's a tie."

"No, Michael," he said, and he gave out a long sigh. "It's an example of two basic emotions—pity and lust."

The audience roared with laughter.

—*Michael Douglas*
Actor, producer, philanthropist

"War Was the Best Thing to Happen to Me"

"In our training, you could qualify as a pilot, navigator or bombardier. I wanted to be a pilot, but didn't make the grade. So I chose bombardier because I got lost easily. I figured all I had to do was drop the bomb for it to hit the ground."
— Larry on his career choices in the Army Air Corps

World War II was the making and almost the unmaking of First Lieutenant Larry Crandell. The experience created opportunities he would not have had otherwise. It also nearly took his life.

There is the story of his plane being shot down and the subsequent award of his Purple Heart medal. There is the story of how he single-handedly wiped out most of the freshwater fish in Germany. We will get to both stories.

But first you should know this: For Larry, going to war meant a quantum leap in the quality of his life. He says, without a hint of exaggeration, that he might never have left his factory job—screwing together big telephone switchboards for Western Electric in Newark—if it hadn't been for the war. Instead, in 1943, he entered a training program for the Army Air Corps, and his life started on a new trajectory.

The tragedy and sacrifice of the war were unavoidable for Larry. Fellow flyers sat next to him at mess hall one day; the next, they were gone— along with their planes—their names to be added to the honor roll, their families to be sent the news they dreaded.

The risk of dying young was significant, but more significant for Larry was the opportunity to transform his life. First, the training he received from the Army Air Corps allowed him to become an officer and then, after he served, to receive an undergraduate education at Syracuse University at the government's expense. By the time he graduated with a B.A. in political science, he was set on a path that would lead him to become a well-paid executive in New York City in the 1950s, living a life that he would have dismissed as a fantasy 10 years before.

"Without the chance to do military service," he says, "I probably wouldn't have risen beyond the assembly line. It might sound odd, but the war was the best thing to happen to me."

It wasn't the safest thing, however. On December 11, 1944, his B-24 bomber went down in the Adriatic Sea. The experience made him religious for the first and probably only time in his life. These are his words.

∽

THE 15TH Air Force flew out of Italy. We had it relatively easy compared to the 8th Air Force, which flew out of England. But our planes still got shot down. We had maybe 15 percent casualties. It was enough to keep you alert.

The two toughest targets for us were Munich and Vienna. On this day we were headed for Vienna. The city was heavily armed. They had batteries of four 88-millimeter anti-aircraft guns, so the shots were in sequence. *Pum, pum, pum, pum.* Puffs of black smoke far below. You couldn't hear anything. When you're enclosed in glass, as the bombardier is, you just see them. You'd wait for the fourth puff. You knew the guns meant potential death. They were frightening. And fascinating.

You need to understand, we were slow-moving targets. We flew B-24s. One of the uncomplimentary names for the B-24 was the "pregnant footlocker." It had a large underbelly, and a top speed of 160 miles per hour. We'd lose a race with most European sports cars now.

On that day we ran into some fighter opposition and two of our four engines were shot out over Vienna, which of course was in the grasp of German power at the time.

Now, B-17 bombers flew beautifully on two engines. The B-24 did not. With only two engines working, it wasn't a matter of whether we would crash, but when. Fortunately, we had a very able pilot. He kept us aloft for as long as he could, and then he announced we were going to ditch. That means a plane that's designed to land on terra firma is going down in the water.

We braced ourselves. I was initially pleased we were going to crash into water, which in my experience certainly seemed softer than land. That notion was sharply dispelled by the massive "clunk" as we made contact with the Adriatic—by that time we were going 100 mph. The force was tremendous. I momentarily blacked out.

When I came to, I was underwater. I thought: I'm not a bad swimmer. Funny the thoughts you have. I was 21 years old. I thought: I'm certainly not a good swimmer, but it would be odd if I drowned.

Then I stood up.

You see, I was still in the airplane, in three feet of water. You can drown in two inches of water if your nose is covered. But I had recovered consciousness. So I didn't have to swim to safety, I just climbed out. In fact, all ten of the crew climbed out before the plane sank. That was fortunate because the B-24's floating ability was very poor.

The crew sprang the yellow dinghies, and we sat in them in the water. In December, the water is like it is off Santa Barbara—50 to 55 degrees Fahrenheit. So we sat in the dinghies for two hours until we were picked up by an Italian fishing boat and taken to land. An Army truck picked us up. (The Air Corps was part of the Army.) The truck took us to Foggia, about 20 or 30 miles away.

I had suffered a bump on the head. It was treated quickly. But then they woke me up at 2:00 in the morning and presented me with the Purple Heart.

My head healed quickly—I still have a little scar. But that wasn't the end of the story. You see, I developed the condition for which Preparation H was created. To put it bluntly, I had the piles. When I got back to the squadron, I had to go for treatment to the same clinic that looked after those suffering from venereal disease. Venereal disease was a major problem. There were signs all over. I must say that as a good officer I followed instructions where V.D. was concerned. Mainly because I couldn't get within arm's length of a woman.

The word spread, however, that Lieutenant Crandell had venereal disease because I went to the same place for treatment as the V.D. sufferers.

I dubbed it the immaculate infection.

A Memorable Presence

I STARTED thinking back over all the community and charitable events that Dilling and I have attended at which Larry has been such a memorable presence. Whether serving as master of ceremonies, auctioneer or distinguished guest, he is always the life of the party. People are drawn to him not only for his enthusiasm and infectious good humor, but also for his sincere interest in people and his heartfelt compassion for others. He has helped countless charitable groups to raise much-needed funds for programs that directly benefit the people of our local communities and our society. Many, many lives have been changed for the better as a result of his philanthropic vision and his tireless devotion.

—Henry Yang
Chancellor, University of California at Santa Barbara

Missing Munich

Larry's crash landing and his Purple Heart didn't end his military service overseas. He flew a total of 35 missions—his first in August 1944, and his last in March 1945. In January of that year, only a month after being shot down, he was under way once more—this time to bomb Munich. Here is his version of the story.

MUNICH was one of the most heavily fortified German cities. It is in southern Germany, and because we were stationed down near the heel of Italy, Munich was about at the limit of our range. The trip took six to seven hours. We were leading the squadron that was leading the group. The squadron had seven or eight airplanes, and the group had four squadrons, so there were about 30 airplanes in all. The radar operator, nicknamed the "mickey operator" for some reason, was in the lead plane of the lead squadron. That was the plane I was in, well on my way to a captaincy, which is two silver bars as opposed to the one silver bar of a first lieutenant.

As we approached the target, it appeared to be 90 percent undercast. (On the ground we think of the weather being "overcast," but up in the sky we called it "undercast.") That meant we had 10 percent visibility. We turned on the initial point, which was 15 to 25 miles from the target. That's when the pilot turns the actual steering of the plane over to the bombardier. The steering mechanism was connected to the bomb sight, so when you turned the sight the plane turned with it.

There was an emergency switch called the "toggle switch," and only two people had access to it, the bombardier and the mickey operator. Standard operating procedure was to uncover it as you turned on the initial point. As we did, I was fighting to see the ground so I could home in on the target.

That's when either the radar operator or I hit the toggle switch.

Unfortunately, we were still 22 miles away from the target.

Normally, there was a certain dark beauty to the way the bombs came out sequentially. Every second or two. But when the toggle switch was hit, the bombs were released all at the same time. That is to say, we had ten 500-pound bombs, and they were all dumped at once.

Following normal procedure, all the planes dropped their bombs after ours.

I always tell people that the bombs landed in a big lake and Germany was without fish for weeks. But in reality the cloudy weather meant I couldn't see where they landed.

The pilot then radioed back one of the great historic messages of World War II: "Mission failure, reasons other than weather."

As we flew back over northern Italy, I prayed that we would be shot down. I didn't want to be killed, but I didn't want to go back either.

As we taxied to a stop, a brigadier general stood outside. He braced me and said, "Attention, Lieutenant." I snapped to attention. He said, "What's the reason for the terrible mission?" Or words to that effect. I said, "No excuse, sir."

After a mission, it was customary for intelligence officers to debrief each member of each air crew. "Did you see anything? Did this burn? Do you think we hit the target? Were there enemy fighters?" This time they had an interrogation more suited to the grilling of public enemy number one. Me.

In the long run, intelligence cannot cover up for stupidity and I began my *mea culpa*. To this day I don't know which one of us hit the toggle switch. But one thing is sure, it was inadvertent.

With all the planes dropping their bombs, someone calculated that the botched mission cost the government $35,000—in 1945 dollars! The next day I was back flying a mission—but I had dropped from the lead plane to the 28th. I think the idea was that if I screwed up I might mislead a few swallows, but no airplanes.

The captaincy never came through. I flew the rest of my missions in ignominious obscurity.

Larry is fond of telling self-deprecating stories. His story of missing Munich by 22 miles is factual, but it hardly sums up his military career. His official military record at the time of his discharge from active duty, June 4, 1945, tells a different story. It notes his decorations and citations as the following:

European-African-Middle East Theater Campaign Ribbon

Air Medal with Three Bronze Oak Leaf Clusters

Distinguished Flying Cross

Purple Heart

Just One of the Girls

THERE are a few people you meet in your life who leave indelible footprints on your heart. Larry Crandell is one of those people. I'd like to share one of my favorite indelible moments—I call them Crandell-ible moments.

You think of our tall and strapping Larry as a real he-man type. Well, I think of him as just one of the girls. I remember hosting a Valentine's Day luncheon at the Montecito Inn more than 10 years ago. Somehow Larry got wind of my event and crashed the party. He came in armed with red roses for every woman at our table and sat down to chat all the way through the dessert course. These were the good old days when Larry was eating dessert, of course. My mother was among the guests, and she still talks about that handsome man who came to lunch and never left. The man who made us all feel so special.

—Anne Smith Towbes
Philanthropist and owner of KEYT-TV

Defining Success

IN *HAMLET,* Shakespeare gave this line of advice to the pompous windbag Polonius: "Neither a borrower nor a lender be."

Larry couldn't disagree more. He borrows and lends with abandon. Not money. His main trade is in words and wisdom. He says he's never had an original thought in his life. Though he's using hyperbole to make a point, the statement is largely true. One of Larry's most potent secrets is that he builds on the wisdom of those who have preceded him—constructing his edifice of life from the designs of people who have gone before.

Larry finds the great American man of letters, Ralph Waldo Emerson, particularly inspiring. Larry jokes that when he went to school with Ralph no one would have guessed how brilliant the Emerson kid would turn out.

But in seriousness, Larry holds Emerson's definition of success close to his heart. The fit with Larry's *modus vivendi* is uncanny. Here is Emerson's answer to the question, "What is success?"

> *To laugh often and much, to win the respect of intelligent people, the affection of children, and the appreciation of honest critics, to endure the betrayal of false friends, to appreciate beauty, to find the best in others, to leave the world a bit better whether by a healthy child, a garden patch or a redeemed social condition. To know that even one life has breathed easier because you have lived, that is to have succeeded.*

Syracuse University and Basketball

FOR LARRY, one of the best things about the war was coming home.

He remembers seeing the riot of color in the schoolyard as children played in the spring of 1945. Compared to the impoverished, war-impacted landscape of Italy, it seemed like a blossoming of humanity. "Yellows, purples, greens, whites," Larry says, recalling the view from the train as he traveled near Boston. "I realized that for the previous nine months I had lived in a gray world." The colors of the playground and the happy kids became a metaphor for the end of the war. "There were these kids far from danger. Playing. Just being kids." He felt elated by the sight.

It was only the first of many pleasant aspects of the homecoming. "I don't remember girls liking me at all," Larry said. "Then I went back to my old employer, Western Electric, right after I got back from the war. There was a large room filled with a hundred assemblers. They were all women. I walked down and a buzz started and the whistling started. Now, I think Quasimodo would have gotten a warm reception because of the sense of patriotism. [Larry was in uniform.] Still, it felt great."

When Larry returned to Syracuse to pursue his bachelor's degree—he had done some of his pre-military training there before going overseas—he encountered another strange situation. In June 1945, when he began the summer session, he was one of only 17 male students at Syracuse. There were about 3,000 female students.

"And I still couldn't make out," he says.

But he could play basketball. Basketball was something he had loved since he was a child. In fact, when he was a teenager he switched churches in Newark, technically converting from a Methodist to a Presbyterian, because the latter church had a much better gymnasium.

At the age of 22, Larry was a very mature freshman and stepped right into a starting role for Syracuse. By the time he was a senior, he says, he had worked his way to sixth man. The return of other servicemen from the war increased the competition considerably.

Larry describes the period as one of the happiest in his life. He studied political science, but according to his own account he was far from a diligent student, compiling a "C" average. Still, he was seen as a leader. In only his first autumn semester at Syracuse he was invited to become a "student dean." He looked after 17 other students, and for that he received room and board. (His tuition was already taken care of by the government.)

As a student dean, Larry's job was to start each meal. One time he asked a professor to say grace. The rather prissy man stood and said, "Please bless this food to our use. And us to thy fateful service. *For Christ's sake!* Amen." The emphasis and the cadence of the delivery made the blessing sound blasphemous, not to mention inadvertently comic. "*For Christ's sake*" was a common way at the time to take the Lord's name in vain. As student dean, Larry suddenly found himself in a new role: trying to stifle the snickers of the undergraduates who found the graceless grace the most entertaining thing they'd heard in quite some time.

Larry loved everything about being at college—the value put on intelligence, the company of smart people and of course the chance to play basketball at the inter-collegiate level. "I adored the camaraderie," he says. "Running out to the band playing. Reading the accounts of the games in the paper. Because I didn't play in high school, I was thrilled to wear 'Syracuse' across my chest."

The team traveled around the eastern United States playing games. Larry has vivid memories of playing in Madison Square Garden—where he once put up a shot with such force that it sailed over the basket *and the backboard.* A wag in the crowd hollered, "Shut the windows!" and the ball landed in the lap of a startled spectator.

Or so goes the story as he tells it.

By now, you've probably caught on; but just in case, here's a *caveat lector*—let the reader beware. One must always allow for some degree of embellishment when listening to the stories Larry tells about himself.

"I tell the truth as I feel it plays best," he once told me.

However, the embellishment usually works in reverse of normal expectation. He exaggerates his faults and foibles rather than his successes. We hear about the fish killed by the mistaken release of bombs. We hear about the shot so bad it landed in a co-ed's lap. Larry's stories are often humorous, but there is a deeper reason for the way in which he spins his yarns.

Here's an example from Syracuse days. "I ran for junior class president in 1948," he recalls. "I spent my spare time in the student union playing bridge and talking with people. I was on the basketball team. I felt that I was a shoo-in and so I didn't campaign much. I got walloped in the vote."

Even back then, Larry turned the defeat into a focal point. After losing the vote, the first thing he talked about with his fellow students was his inability to attract enough support and his misplaced confidence. This was "Larry irony" at work. Using his frailty as a strength, his defeat becomes an illustration not of failure, but of how he copes with disappointment.

"There's something in me that abhors sympathy if it tips over into pity," he says. "So I make fun of myself. 'Did you see Crandell? Doesn't he look silly? Did you hear him get mixed up in the middle of his speech?' I don't want to tell people my troubles. Everybody likes sympathy, but I prefer adulation, admiration, approval."

By honestly and humorously pointing out his own shortcomings, Larry leaves the way open for others to give him the praise he so enjoys. You might accuse him of being self-serving, but that is far too simple a description. Larry often seeks and gets what he wants, but he does so in ways that let others join the fun. The benefit is mutual. He stoops to conquer and is, in turn, conquered by others' recognition.

You smile. He smiles. It's the perfect happy ending for Larry.

Adulation, admiration, approval. Call it Larry's top rating—the Triple-A.

Keeping Score

I MET Larry Crandell playing basketball at the Goleta Boys & Girls Club about 25 years ago. I remember his two-hand set shot that went in almost every time. I remember that he never passed the ball and that he was a pretty good rebounder. He always guarded me, but I was just too quick for him and I would play very hard. When I found out that Larry was 20 years older than me, I felt guilty and decided to let up and actually let him score. When the scoreboard at the club went down because of his scoring, I asked Larry to help raise the money to buy a new one. He hit up all the adult players, and we had a new scoreboard.

—Sal Rodriguez
Executive director, United Boys & Girls Clubs
of Santa Barbara County

The Guns of Navarone

SOME TIME ago, around 1986, Larry Crandell walked onto a basketball court with a blinding flash of whiteness and earned a nickname. He wore white tennis shorts, a paper-thin white shirt, white socks and white sneakers—all of the bleached attire blending with his faded white skin. In a dark gym, Larry was a walking whiteout.

This pale hoop player, angular and bony, began his warm-ups by working out his mouth. Larry yammered incessantly, seemingly paid by the syllable. He squeezed in jokes between the thump of the basketball and the squeal of shoes on the gym floor.

"What University you graduate from, Paul?

"University of Southern California," I answered.

"Sorry to hear that. It explains a lot."

Once the game began, Larry mainly ran around the perimeter of the floor, letting younger, bigger bodies do the banging under the hoop. He waited for his chance on offense, a teammate to drive, often me. He looked for someone to kick a pass out to his outstretched arms.

Larry caught. Then he launched. He looked like a rickety cannon, slightly bent forward, his base unstable. With a sudden fling, the ball arched toward the basket, bringing to mind a lob from heavy artillery, perhaps stationed in a cliff-side bunker. After the ball was released, Larry's arms twitched backward, a sort of human ballistic recoil. The shot fell through the hoop.

"Look at that," I chuckled. "You're 'The Guns of Navarone.'"

Most amazing, Larry played the whole session—almost two hours of calorie-annihilating, full-court basketball.

I could only fantasize what it would be like to be as active as Larry as the decades stack up. By my calculations, on Larry's nickname-earning day, "The Guns of Navarone" was 62 years old.

—*Paul Vercammen*
Former news director, KEYT-TV

"Over My Dead Body"—
The Essence of Brotherly Love

Larry's time at Syracuse was made even more joyful by the matriculation of his youngest brother, Martin, during Larry's last year. At that time, Martin was a magnificent athlete and an indifferent student. He also held his older brother in very high regard. I'll let Larry take up the story:

❧

THE YEAR, 1947. The place, Syracuse University. The time, September, a couple of weeks after beginning what would be my senior year.

I finished the course work in three years by taking classes during the summers. Actually, work is the wrong word. Put in three years, got a degree. That's more like it.

My brother, Martin Chester Crandell, had just started his first year. He was an excellent boxer. Quite athletic. In Newark, he had won the Five-High-School title in high hurdles and the discus. One hundred eighty-eight pounds, six-foot-one. In boxing, he won the novice division of Golden Gloves. Loy Simmons, a legend as the boxing coach at Syracuse, spotted him. Martin received the only boxing scholarship Syracuse offered. The whole family was proud of him.

He came to me after maybe 10 days of the semester, and of course, I was joyous at the prospect of having my young brother on campus. But he was *not* happy.

"Lawrence," he said, "I'm going home. I can't cut it."

"Did you get a bad grade?" I said.

" I haven't gotten any grades," he said. "I just know the work is too difficult."

I had a flair for the dramatic. I looked him square in the eye and pulled myself to my full six-foot-three inches in height.

"You're going home over my dead body."

He shrugged and said, "Hey, if that's the way you want it."

I was much the better talker, but he could have knocked me cold with a single blow.

I immediately changed tactics. "You're gonna hurt Mom so much," I said. "She's so proud of what you've accomplished. Why don't you wait until you get a grade? You haven't gotten a grade or exam back yet."

He grudgingly agreed to stay at Syracuse until he got his first grade.

A few days later, he came back fuming. "You son of a bitch."

"Hey," I said. "Easy. You're insulting Mom. What's wrong? Did you flunk something?"

"No," he said. "I got an A on an English paper!"

I was dumbfounded. Not a common experience for me. After a moment or two, I asked him why he was so angry.

"Because you fixed the grade."

Now, honesty forces me to say that I was a bit of a big man on campus. All the ex-veterans were. And I *was* on the varsity basketball team.

"You fixed it," he repeated.

"Marty," I sighed for effect. "What's my grade point average?"

"Two-point-zero-something."

"Don't you think that while I was in there fixing your grade I'd have given myself a little bump—maybe up to a B?"

His forehead wrinkled. He looked down.

I told him I thought he had earned it. I told him my reputation might help him in some areas, but not in academics. I told him I thought he could make it on his own. I told him I had faith in him.

He stayed at Syracuse and went on to graduate. And though he wasn't a particularly distinguished scholar, he was very hard-working—the antithesis of his big brother Lawrence. Later, he went to law school at night to get his degree, and later still, he studied at and received his master's in law from New York University. He became a very successful partner in a prominent law firm.

Oh, and he also won the NCAA Heavyweight Boxing Championship.

When I think of my career at Syracuse, my number-one accomplishment had nothing to do with anything I actually did in the classroom or on the basketball court.

The best thing I did was just to convince Marty to stay in school.

Touché

I HAVEN'T spoken to Larry in 10 years.
  Nothing's the matter. I just didn't want to interrupt him.

—Marcy Crandell
quoted in the Santa Barbara News-Press, *1994*

Dance and Romance

AFTER graduating from Syracuse, Larry spent a brief time in upstate New York selling a revolutionary new synthetic detergent called Tide for Proctor & Gamble. But it wasn't for him, and Larry came home to Newark in 1948. He moved back in with his mother in her small apartment and almost immediately began to miss the college life.

"There were so many things that I enjoyed about Syracuse," he told me in 1986 when I recorded some oral history interviews with him. "In fact, regarding college life in general, there are only two improvements I can think of—one, removing the books and, two, removing the teachers. Lose those two things and you have the perfect environment."

Back in Newark, he began to peruse the newspapers as he considered his next career move. One advertisement caught his eye. It said you could own your own business if you could learn to dance. It sounded like fun.

There were only two problems. The first was that Larry had never danced. The second was that when Larry went in to apply, the head of the dance business, a man named Arthur Murray, said Larry was the clumsiest applicant for a dance teacher they'd ever had.

But neither problem was insurmountable. You see, Larry liked the atmosphere at the Arthur Murray studio. It was located in the heart of Manhattan, at 43rd and Madison.

"I found the operation glamorous," he said. "Dance studios are mostly mirrors. If I wasn't already narcissistic, I sure got the hang of it in a hurry. There were pretty girls and attractive guys. Everyone was dressed to the nines. People were charming in the way La Belle Charm School people are charming. Surface. Which is probably better than being rotten inside *and* outside."

The way they explained it to Larry, he had to go through an

unpaid period of six weeks as he learned how to dance. After that, he would earn two dollars an hour—which he thought was very good pay.

For a man to learn to dance well enough to teach, he must learn the woman's part as well as his own. Conversely, women teachers must learn the man's part. This was standard for the dance business. But a group of women in Larry's training class asked if they could be excused from having to lead Larry. He was so large and clumsy, they feared for their feet.

Despite the steep learning curve, Larry passed the course and became a teacher. It was the beginning of more than 12 years in the Arthur Murray dance business. It was also a fateful turn of events for Larry personally.

In the teacher training class that started a month after Larry's, there was a woman who didn't fit the normal mold. To be sure, she was trim and good-looking like the other teachers. But whereas many of the other teachers were bubbly and gushy, she was reserved. Whereas many of the teachers were in between show business jobs or aspired to be in showbiz, she was a graduate student studying Shakespeare. Larry puts it this way: "In an environment that was pretty fast and pretty amoral, here was a citadel of quality and straight arrow. I thought she was beautiful."

Her name was Marcy Novak, and she was working on her Ph.D. at Columbia.

Unfortunately, she paid Larry no attention at all. She turned down several requests for a date. Larry remembers, "I said to myself: How could this otherwise intelligent girl resist my charming approach? I thought she was beautiful, but she wasn't impressed with me at all. She didn't say it, but I think she thought I was loud and shallow. So when I finally convinced her to go out with me, I dazzled her. I took her to Walgreen's—which was a drug-store on Times Square. Never being one to stint, I bought her a large Coke. In the weeks to come, I sprang for the occasional 15-cent ice cream sundae. I was determined to help her realize that I was not the cheap, baggy-pants comedian that I appeared to be."

What broke through Marcy's initial reluctance? With his tongue firmly in cheek, Larry says, "Charm. Pure, unadulterated charm." Then in a more thoughtful vein, he adds, "When someone was so interested in her, even Marcy would have her interest piqued a little bit."

After the dates at Walgreens, Larry would walk Marcy to the subway station, but he did not accompany her all the way home. This was a mistake. "I didn't find out until later, but she was angry with me. Subway stations weren't particularly safe then, nor were they as dangerous as they have become. It was probably a thoughtless thing to do. But I had an hour and a half to go home [the commute back to Newark], and if I had taken *her* home, I would have met myself going to work the next day."

But her anger didn't last. The courtship extended onto the dance floor. At Arthur Murray, each student had an instructor, but there were twenty couples dancing in one ballroom. "Because I could lead my partner where I wanted, I would follow Marcy around the dance floor and give her a few visual woo-woos. And when the students left, I would chide her about how closely she danced with her partners."

After a few months, they fell in love. Yet they had to face a separation. She left for the summer to work at a resort at Lake Champlain in upstate New York. When she came back, she wrote Larry a love poem. "I can't remember a word," he says, "but it breaks my heart to think of it. I immediately crumbled into five thousand pieces, quickly reassembled myself, and asked her to marry me."

Larry says he had concluded a long time before that Marcy would be a fine partner. "The best running mate, the best mother, the most loyal wife."

But it wasn't Marcy's steadfast, "classy" qualities that made him pop the question. It was her poem that prompted the proposal and began a union that so far has lasted 56 years and produced five children, nine grandchildren, and two great-grand-children.

Heavenly Honeymoon

FORGIVE me if I seem to dwell on my parents' brilliant beginning as a couple. But what writer could pass up a story about a potentially endless honeymoon.

Larry, of course, had been stationed in Italy during the war, but when the newlywed Crandells flew to Bermuda in 1950 for their honeymoon, it was the first time Marcy had been overseas.

They went in July. The weather was very hot—the vegetation lush and green. They checked into the Castle Harbour Hotel in Tuckerstown. Minutes later, they had rented two bicycles to ride around the 22-mile periphery of Bermuda.

"We went up one hill," says Larry, "and my fanny was dragging. I was red in the face from exhaustion. So we returned the rentals. Traded them in for bicycles with little motors. Thirty miles per hour top speed. But no effort. It was a beautiful, beautiful experience."

The hotel was a venerable building, and their room was lovely. But one of the biggest attractions for the newlywed dancing teachers was the outdoor nightclub.

They danced every night. And swam. And cycled. And shopped. All to the rhythmic accent of Bermudian English, which sounds Caribbean, although Bermuda is off the east coast of North America.

On the last night of their ten-day honeymoon, the hotel manager came up to them and asked Larry and Marcy to extend their stay. He told them that if they would do a 15-minute dance exhibition every night, they could stay as the hotel's guests as long as they wanted.

"The total was $34 a day, including all our meals and room—far beyond our capabilities," remembers Larry. The idea seemed too good to be true, but when Larry wired Mr. Murray to ask for more time off from work, he got the green light. "Mr. Murray said stay another week. We did, and loved it even more because it was free."

Then one night, while they were putting on their dance exhibition, crisis struck. With all the hotel guests gathered round, both sitting at tables and standing, the band struck up a samba. At that exact moment, a large moth dove into Marcy's cleavage. It was disconcerting even for a seasoned dancer like Marcy.

"She froze," says Larry. "It was like dancing with a clumsy truck driver or the truck itself. I hissed at her, 'Relax!' She said she couldn't. There was a bug fluttering down the inside of her dress. But in the best tradition of show business we carried on to the end of the dance. I was miffed, though, because we couldn't do our *botto foco con batuc* [a fancy spiral step]."

The moth did nothing, however, to spoil the halcyon honeymoon.

In fact, Larry and Marcy enjoyed it so much that they returned there in 1958.

Double Dessert

THIS is a favorite technique of the Silver Tongue.

At the end of a lunch with a friend or an associate, Larry often has his guest order two desserts—one for the guest to eat at the table, and one to be boxed up and taken back to the guest's office or home and given to a person of the guest's choosing.

It's leveraged generosity. The way Larry does it, the gift has a three-way benefit:

1. The luncheon guest enjoys choosing who will receive the dessert and delivering it to him or her.

2. The recipient of the boxed dessert gets to enjoy a sweet surprise.

3. Larry gets to enjoy one of his favorite moments—setting in motion a chain reaction of appreciation.

"It extends the good feeling of the lunch and triples the fun," he says. "I especially like doing it for—(a) people who would rarely think of giving such a treat and (b) people who would rarely expect to get one."

The end recipients of the desserts are almost always delighted. They feel grateful to the deliverer, who chose them, as well as to Larry, the purchaser.

The Silver Tongue, of course, never met a word of appreciation he didn't appreciate. So the circle of giving is often completed with Larry on the receiving end.

He's even expanded the concept to the idea of "dessert diplomacy"—advising one nonprofit to cater dessert for the board meeting of an influential group of funders as a gesture of goodwill.

There is almost always irony interwoven in the things Larry does.

This particular technique is no different. You see, Larry has type II diabetes and can't eat dessert himself.

Yet when people ask him how he is, he often answers, "Life is sweet."

His "double dessert" strategy is one reason why.

On Television in the '50s

THE SCREEN was tiny and the pictures were broadcast in black and white, but the impact early television had on America was significant.

The impact on Larry was even more telling.

By 1952, he had become an executive who worked closely with Arthur Murray in the latter's eponymous dance business. When Mr. Murray decided to enter a team in a new pantomime television show produced by CBS, Larry was picked as the "brains" of the team. The other three team members were "three women with *décolletage*," according to Larry. "I had no *décolletage*, but Charades was a fun, quick and easy game for me. And in dance studios, you can be a brain without being a brain."

Called "Say It with Acting," the show's premise was simple—one person was given a title or a common saying, and he or she had to act it out silently while the other three teammates guessed. The other teams appearing on the show came from then-current Broadway plays like *Paint Your Wagon*.

Larry remembers it as "pretty exciting." The excitement grew when the Arthur Murray team won the televised competition for nine consecutive weeks. Nine straight weeks of practice at the studio. Nine straight weeks of getting made up along with the Broadway stars. Nine straight weeks of high-profile success. "Brainy" Larry and his teammates were feeling good.

Then a scandal erupted. "It turned out there were allegations that Mr. Murray was paying the producer of the show $100 a week so that the producer would give us simple charade challenges," says Larry. "We had no idea that in sports parlance 'the dump' was on. Once there was even a hint of scandal, we were dropped immediately."

But it wasn't the end of Larry's television career or the attempts to use the medium to promote the dance business.

"The Arthur Murray Dance Party" was a national weekly show on the Dumont Television Network, which in the 1950s was competing with the likes of CBS, NBC and ABC. Larry and Marcy both appeared on the show as background dancers. You might say they had an appetite for this particular gig. They were paid not in money, but in meal vouchers. They got 30 meal tickets each for every week they were on. The tickets were redeemable at Schrafft's, an upscale restaurant. Larry remembers you could get a complete steak dinner for five dollars there.

"We lived at the restaurant, plus we had the glamour of being on television, and once in a great while a relative would see a show. My mother never missed it on her eight-inch screen."

One of Larry's jobs was to select the young dancers who would appear on the show. In the 1950s there was no videotape, of course. Instead, there were Kinescopes—films of the TV screen itself as a show was broadcast. At great expense, Mr. Murray would have Kinescopes made so that he could watch the Sunday show in his office on Monday afternoon. He and Larry would watch the grainy images and decide which dancers to keep on the show and which would leave to make way for new faces.

The show featured some big stars of the 1950s—Rex Harrison and the Ames Brothers to name a few. But one of the stars turned out to be a problem for Larry. A Czech opera singer named Jarmilla Novotna was a featured guest one week. She was six-feet tall, and all of the show's most accomplished dancers were too short to dance with the towering diva.

Enter six-foot-three Larry to the rescue. "My job was to dance her up close to center stage where the microphone was. There she would sing the last chorus of 'Vilia, Oh Vilia' from *The Merry Widow* [by Franz Lehàr]."

The dancing went beautifully. In fact, the steps were not complicated. Jarmilla was graceful as well as tall. And her singing was flawless. Larry says he felt thrilled after performing with an opera legend.

It wasn't the end of the story, though. Larry still cringes at the memory. "It's a famous song for opera fans, but for me it will live in infamy. You see, when Mr. Murray and I sat down to watch the Kinescope the next day, I saw that after I danced her to center stage, the camera didn't isolate on her. They had the two of us in shot. Someone once said that doing nothing on stage is the most difficult job. I agree. In my mind I wasn't Fred Astaire, I was more Ricardo Montalban. But on the Kinescope, I looked like Fatty Arbuckle."

For some reason, Mr. Murray didn't say anything about that episode, but Larry wasn't so fortunate the next time.

Larry picks up the tale. "Of the 50 male dance teachers, 25 were show dancers between shows. They danced magnificently. The rest of us danced well—extremely well compared to the average dancer—but way below the level of the professionals.

"One Sunday night, both of the five-foot-six show dancers were unavailable, and I had to do the lead in a number called 'Put Your Little Foot.' Even back then they had a zoom lens, and it zeroed in on my feet. I kept time easily. It was a simple step."

Once again, Larry finished the number feeling elated, having performed live on nationwide television. But once again, Monday afternoon and the Kinescope viewing session came around. When the "Put Your Little Foot" number began, there was a close-up of Larry's size 12 brogans. They literally filled the screen—looking more like gunships than "little feet." Larry could see Mr. Murray stiffen. At the end of the number, the ballroom dancing king turned to his young executive and said tersely, "Don't *ever* lift your feet off the floor, Larry."

It was dancing advice Larry never forgot.

But he isn't bitter about the natural abundance of his lowest extremities. His mother, after all, taught him to like his feet and their size. Jane always told him he had "aristocratic" feet—though she offered no reason why. As for the clumsy kid from Newark who learned to move gracefully across the floor in tandem with beautiful women like Marcy, well, Larry prefers to refer openly to the length and breadth of his contact with *terra firma*. When asked what size shoe he wears, he usually answers in his best French accent: *"Petit elephant."*

It should be mentioned that Larry's television career did not end in the 1950s. He revived it in the 1970s by filling in on the local Santa Barbara television station (KEYT) show "Sports with Bertka." (Bill Bertka was Santa Barbara City Parks and Recreation Director at the time and went on to a career coaching and managing in the NBA.)

Later in the 1970s, a very small UHF station began to broadcast from downtown Ventura. The station asked Larry to do a half-hour show on real estate—but there was no money to shoot items outside the studio.

Larry says it was very, very low budget. "The cameraman used to wander in and out of the studio during my show. I guess it didn't hold his attention. During one show, I made a move across the studio floor to a blackboard. Unfortunately, the cameraman wasn't at the camera, so I walked right out of the picture."

Larry, being Larry, continued to talk. He told viewers, who were watching a white wall with nothing in front of it, that "the audio is going to work a little better than the video for a while." Larry then lifted the blackboard and carried it back into the frame, before continuing with his talk on real estate.

"Very few people watched," according to Larry. "When Marcy had something else on the tube, it cut overall viewing numbers by a third."

On the last show, Larry interviewed the entire family on live television. I remember it still. At the age of 14, I didn't feel I had a whole lot of insight into real estate investment, but it was still pretty cool. As I recall, Larry asked me what I thought about property values in the area of Santa Barbara Junior High School, where I was in the ninth grade at the time.

Ashley and the Rest of Us

LARRY and Marcy's family planning was somewhat laissez-faire. Larry affectionately refers to me, the fourth of five children, as an "accident." I prefer "love child in wedlock." But, in any case, I feel deeply appreciative that he and Marcy took the course they did, as my very existence depends on their serendipitous fertility.

The only time Larry says they planned a child was the conception of Leslie, the youngest, in 1965. By that time, of course, both Larry and Marcy were in their forties. After Leslie's birth, they proudly told their friends that they had deliberately decided to add to the family. However, having children in mid-life was still out of the ordinary in the mid-1960s. So, naturally, none of their friends believed them.

For the other four kids, Larry described the procreation strategy as pretty much ad hoc: "Marcy got pregnant, and nine months later we would have a baby." Larry loves these little admissions of what appear to be very personal details—told in a self-effacing way with a twinkle in his eye. But in this case, Larry and Marcy were only doing what most American couples were doing at the time—that is, creating the baby boom.

The five children, who arrived over a span of 14 years, benefited from a home where love was expressed every day in all sorts of ways. Larry says he has never met a more dedicated mother than Marcy—which is saying something when you think of how highly he regards his own mother. As for me, I know I wouldn't trade my upbringing, or all the support I have had from my parents, for anything.

I felt blessed to grow up in my family. My memories span from my dad chasing us around the house as the "Monster of Montecito" to my mother quoting verse from Shakespearian drama in the back yard. Often the family dinner table became the venue for a debate about language. I have strong memories of listening as my father or mother stood at the table to read definitions of strange words from a dictionary the size of an archbishop's Bible.

But here is not the place for me to take what Larry calls "a trip down memory lane." Instead, I want to confine my words to the only one of the Crandell children who has not survived.

My sister Leslie, myself and my brothers Michael and Larry, Jr., are all over 40 now. But the eldest child Ashley, very sadly, never made it to the big 4–0.

Parents are fond of saying that they love all their children. But most mothers and fathers will also admit that the first child has a unique place in their hearts. So it was with Ashley. Born July 6, 1951, she was proof of my parents' ability to be fruitful and multiply in a hurry. Larry, donning the mantle of Puckish mischief, usually tells the story like this: "Marcy and I were married on July the third...Ashley was born July the sixth."

Of course, the marriage was in 1950, and Ashley was born a year later.

Ashley was born in New York City and stayed with her parents in an apartment on the campus of Columbia University. Marcy was working toward her doctorate in English literature at the time. "Marcy found a place in Butler Hall," remembers Larry. "Very nice apartment. The address was 88 Morningside Drive. Down the way, 60 Morningside Drive was occupied by the president of Columbia, a man by the name of Dwight Eisenhower. I don't know what happened to him."

Ashley turned out to be brilliant in both the sciences and the humanities. She was a National Merit Scholar in high school, received an academic scholarship to Stanford University, then a fellowship to do her graduate work at Yale. In her early thirties, she became the editor of a pioneering project in Old English scholarship at the University of Toronto. (Old English was the language spoken in England from roughly 500 A.D. to 1100 A.D. It would be almost unrecognizable to most of us today.) Her job, as she described it, was like being a detective—piecing together the rare existing written examples of Old English (from wills, charters, recipes, etc.) and finding their precise meanings. The main problem is that while today we are used to seeing language written in all sorts of ways, Old English was almost entirely a spoken language.

Ashley was a shining star. As humble as she was talented, she disliked public attention and preferred to work out of the limelight. (Definitely not Larry's genes at work there.) But she did have Larry's big heart and an enormous capacity for compassion that made her feel the pain of others—almost viscerally—no matter how distant they were.

She died before she reached her 38th birthday. She left a hole in all our hearts. But my parents felt it in a way no others did. To lose a child before her time was devastating. Marcy and Larry were emotionally and physically stricken.

Her photo, and that of her then-husband Bruce Amos, still stands on my father's desk at work. Ashley is in the foreground smiling, perhaps a little self-conscious that she is the main subject of the shot. Bruce looks on with devotion from the background. It was taken at their wedding reception in 1976—held in my parent's backyard. I know my father looks at it every day and is moved by the memory of the beauty of her spirit.

In 1986, I recorded a series of interviews with Larry as oral history to save for his grandchildren and their descendants. The interviews have proved very helpful in the writing of this book. But on one particular March afternoon, we didn't talk about nonprofits or sports or even Larry's favorite subject (himself). That day, we talked about Ashley. It was three years *before* her death. This is what Larry said:

"She was an easy child to love. Very serious, very sincere. That's the kind of adult she is. She turned into one of the most caring persons I've ever met.

"I am in awe of her, and I love her and admire her. She's loyal. She's sacrificing to the nth degree—and I mean that in the best meaning of the word. There is no martyr in her. She's just tremendously giving.

"She also has a feeling for her mother that is very rare. They have a beautiful relationship. She loves Marcy very much. A deep and permanent love.

"For my birthday, when she was 11, she memorized a poem called 'The Highwayman' [by Alfred Noyes]. Early on, I asked you kids to give something of yourselves rather than buy a gift. To listen to her recite the poem was just a joyous experience. 'Tlot-Tlot.' It's one of the greatest gifts I've ever gotten."

The poem, at 17 stanzas and 104 lines, is of considerable length—especially for an 11 year-old to memorize. Here is how it begins:

> *The wind was a torrent of darkness among the gusty trees,*
> *The moon was a ghostly galleon tossed upon cloudy seas,*
> *The road was a ribbon of moonlight over the purple moor,*
> *And the highwayman came riding—*
> > *Riding—riding—*
> *The highwayman came riding, up to the old inn door.*

And here is the stanza Larry referred to:

> *Tlot tlot, tlot tlot! Had they heard it? The horse-hoofs,*
> > *ringing clear;*
> *Tlot tlot, tlot tlot, in the distance! Were they deaf that they*
> > *did not hear?*
> *Down the ribbon of moonlight, over the brow of the hill,*
> *The highwayman came riding—*
> > *Riding—riding—*
> *The redcoats looked to their priming! She stood up straight*
> > *and still.*

The poem, which tells of the ill-fated love between a highwayman and a young woman, is both heroic and tragic. Ashley's life could also be described with both those terms. But on Larry's birthday back in 1963, there was only joy. As he sat and listened to his daughter recite the verses she'd learned by heart, he was truly happy.

It may seem a digression to write so much about Ashley in this book. But to honor her is to honor Larry. At age 11, she listened to what he asked for and gave of herself. That she chose to give words makes sense. What could make a better present for a silver tongue? To remember her love of language is to pay homage to the rich heritage of words that Larry and Marcy provided for all us children.

My personal sadness at Ashley's loss is matched only by my deep sense of appreciation that she was my sister and that we were both the offspring of parents who loved both wisely and well.

The Master of Hope

IRVIN D. Yalom, M.D., the existential therapist, said the greatest thing you can give someone is hope.

I call Larry Crandell the Master of Hope because he understands and uses the principle Yalom teaches.

A capital fundraising project was failing because few people believed in the success of the project. I invited the principal players to meet Larry at the Moby Dick restaurant for breakfast. It was there, over sunny-side-up eggs, coffee for four and one Diet Coke, that a plan for raising $6 million took shape.

I watched doubt turn to hope right before my eyes. After that initial meeting, committees were created, press packets designed and Larry became the voice of the capital campaign. The $6 million was raised, and the charity blossomed. Remarkably, it all happened without having a strong base of cultivated donors.

As a marriage and family therapist, I have seen once-despairing clients begin a process of change and healing. The discovery of hope is often the turning point.

Larry creates hope with every project he takes under his wing. Hope is his gift.

—Marsha Marcoe, MFT
Corporate liaison, Donald Bren School of
Environmental Science and Management,
University of California at Santa Barbara

Santa Barbara—Love at First Sunlight

LARRY has a standard line about the house in Santa Barbara where he and Marcy have lived for more than four decades.

"We paid $48,500 for it in 1960," he says. "Since then, we've poured at least 150 bucks into maintenance and improvements. Now, 46 years later, we owe more than $200,000. That's what I call appreciation."

The humor hides a long-term love affair he has had with the house and with Santa Barbara itself.

With four children in tow, Larry and Marcy moved from Pennsylvania to the San Francisco Bay Area in the late 1950s. They then decided to move to Santa Barbara. Larry purchased the Montecito house in June of 1960—in the Hedgerow area off San Ysidro Road. Larry now refers to the neighborhood as "Baja Montecito."

"It was very much an adventure because I selected the house without Marcy seeing it. It was built in what was called a 'contemporary style'—about 2,400 to 2,500 square feet, with cathedral ceilings and large window walls. I must confess I loved it then and I love it now. But if someone gave me truth serum and made me talk of its weaknesses, I would say that the heating system was designed by someone who spent his whole life in equatorial Africa. The bedroom portion of the house has regular height ceilings, unlike the entry, the dining room, and the living room. The thermostat, unfortunately, is in the living room. So when it's 60 degrees in the living room, it's usually 80 degrees in the bedroom."

Larry's main reason for buying this particular house actually had nothing to do with its heating or style. He was under strict instructions from Marcy to make sure the house was in a good school district. On that account, he did very well. Larry is proud to point out that a total of nine of his children and grandchildren have graduated from Montecito Union School.

"I like the sense of roots," Larry told the *Santa Barbara News-Press* in 2003. "Nothing is more fun than a sense of belonging, being attached. As long as I've been here, I still want to grab people by the lapels and tell them what a wonderful place this is. It's the same reason I never travel. Where could I find any place better than this?"

When Larry first got to Santa Barbara, he felt that any time the sun was out it was a "mortal sin" to be indoors. "I just couldn't work. In Harrisburg it was sunny maybe six days a year. Here, even when the day dawned foggy, by 10 or 11 A.M., it would be beautiful. Solid hours of perfect weather. I got the first tan of my life."

Not bad for the former first lieutenant who was so pale-skinned that during World War II he was sent to see a medic after suffering a severe case of sunburn. Of course, in those days, exposing your skin to the sun was thought to be healthy. In the 1980s, however, Larry developed what he calls a "slight case of melanoma." He stays out of the sun now if he can, but he is far from disappointed. "I never wanted my skin or my teeth to outlast me," he says. "And I've been pleased a thousand times that we moved here."

For the boy from inner-city Newark, sunny Santa Barbara just may be the dream fulfillment of the song he learned in Sunday school as a boy. It's a song he has never forgotten and still performs—with hand gestures—for his children and grandchildren.

> *Climb, climb up Sunshine Mountain,*
> *Heavenly breezes blow.*
> *Climb, climb up Sunshine Mountain,*
> *Faces all aglow.*
> *Turn, turn your hearts from doubting,*
> *Looking to the sky.*
> *Climb, climb up Sunshine Mountain,*
> *You and I.*

Start by Liking People

"YOU have it in your power to increase the sum total of the world's happiness. How? By giving a few words of sincere appreciation to someone who is lonely or discouraged. Perhaps you will forget tomorrow the kind words you say today, but the recipient may cherish them over a lifetime."

Dale Carnegie wrote that, and once Larry heard it, he adopted it as his creed.

As I've mentioned before, Larry sees no shame in borrowing wisdom from others. In fact, he believes that "ideas are impersonal. They visit some of us for a short time, then get passed on to somebody else." This sharing of ideas goes both ways. Larry is flattered if someone uses one of his ideas, attributed or not, and he is the first to incorporate someone else's good idea or joke into his own "dog-and-pony show."

Larry has adopted several such ideas from Dale Carnegie.

Carnegie wrote a book called *How to Win Friends and Influence People* in 1936. Since then, the book has sold 30 million copies. Carnegie built a business training people in self-improvement, sales, interpersonal relationships and public speaking. The online encyclopedia *Wikipedia* writes that "one of the core ideas in his books is that it is possible to change other people's behavior by changing one's reaction to them."

Larry and Marcy took the Dale Carnegie course in 1958. Since then, Larry has become known for reacting creatively to people, for cutting through social niceties to establish a connection. When he first meets someone, he has the ability to make that person feel comfortable and to draw them out. He often has them laughing or smiling within a minute. Even with strangers, he can foster a genuine sense of warmth and acceptance in a short amount of time.

The irony is that he makes them feel safe by almost never playing if safe himself. He loves to rib other men. "Always tease someone about their strong points," he says. And he loves to talk relationships with women.

Some of the philosophy that grounds Larry's approach comes straight from Dale Carnegie. "His thesis was simple," says Larry. "Start by liking people, show them you like them, and you'll get liked back."

One of the ways Larry shows his affection for people is to ask them to talk about things that matter to them.

When he meets a couple, he often begins by focusing on their relationship. A typical conversation might go like this (and remember, Larry has just met these people):

Larry: Are you together?

Woman: Yes, we're married.

Larry: How long?

Man: Twelve years.

Larry (with real interest): How's it going?

At this point, there is usually an electric silence as husband and wife react to Larry and the question. Although we are accustomed to being asked about how we are, asking a couple about a marriage is anything but common. In fact, most couples would find it too personal—especially during an introduction. That's why Larry asks, "How's it going?" He wants to break down the walls of formality while relying on his *bonhomie* to reassure people. Laughter is often the result—especially from the husband. There usually follows light-hearted, friendly banter.

At some point, the couple usually says *pro forma* that things are going well in their marriage. But by then, the unexpected question has done its job. It has melted the ice and, together with Larry's innate playfulness, opened the door to a little fun.

One of Larry's other favorite techniques is to ask a couple how they met. Larry finds the stories interesting, but it's often the couple who enjoy the exchange most—reciting the story of their courtship in detail. By asking how two people became a couple, Larry establishes some intimacy early on, gets an insight into the people he's meeting and allows them to tell a story about something they know really well (another Dale Carnegie tenet).

In a way, it's formulaic. Larry will ask the same question of any couple at any age. But each couple has a different story to tell, and so the result is individualized. In the end, Larry's one-size-fits-all approach creates a custom-fit social garment. What would otherwise be an exchange of plodding pleasantries often becomes a very personal, enjoyable interplay.

At the heart of this approach is Larry's almost universal affection for others. He often teases people, but usually about areas where they feel secure, and never in a mean-spirited way. When he asks them a question, they feel he likes them. (He does.) And more often than not, they begin to feel that they like him, too.

Business Adventures

LARRY sometimes waxes philosophical. And nothing makes him more philosophical than recollecting his business career.

"Sometimes we forget," says Larry, "for every disaster, there is usually a catastrophe just waiting to happen."

Of course, Larry has had numerous successes in business. Still, what strikes the observer first about Larry's voyage of enterprise is not so much the treasure he's amassed, but how many ports he's visited.

In the 1950s, Larry's career with the Arthur Murray company blossomed, and he ended up owning studio franchises in Philadelphia, Harrisburg, San Francisco and eventually Santa Barbara. But in the 1960s, ballroom dancing ceased to be the important social tool it once was, and Larry found himself on the beautiful South Coast—with a tan, four children and no job.

So he decided to get entrepreneurial. That's not surprising. Larry's always been creative. But those who know him well will be surprised that he chose to go into the health food business.

To put this in context, you must understand that for most of his life Larry defined a complete meal as:

1. A doughnut
2. A bowl (or carton) of ice cream
3. A Hershey's bar and/or potato chips
4. A 16-ounce Pepsi.

"Since I don't drink or smoke, I had to focus my vices on food," Larry told the *Santa Barbara News-Press* in 1985. "I was the kind of guy who had to see the bottom of the Dreyer's ice cream carton. I'd eat a quart, a quart and a half, in one sitting. I loved sweets and oily things."

Still, he disregarded his personal dietary preferences when he saw an opportunity to invest in a protein drink called Nutra-bio.

Unfortunately, few consumers saw the same opportunity. Larry ended up with no return on his investment and a garage full of protein powder. No wonder we Crandell kids grew so tall.

In 1962, Larry became even more lateral in his thinking. He applied for a job as a milkman. His reasoning was straightforward, if not terribly subtle. He told himself that he had always liked to get up early in the morning, so the Derbiano Dairy job should be a good fit. "The guy I interviewed with was very nice," remembers Larry. "He said in all their years they never had a college graduate apply for a job delivering milk."

Larry thought he was a shoo-in.

He wasn't.

Afterwards, with his spirits at an all-time low, he stopped looking for work. It was Marcy who pulled him out of the depression.

"Marcy was almost uniformly supportive of me when things were going poorly. She is so true blue."

She convinced him to study to get a real estate sales license. He agreed, but only on the condition that she study with him. "A friend of mine once defined real estate as a business you fail into. The average person entering real estate is often middle-aged. And I was drifting."

He and Marcy both passed the course—Marcy scored 100 percent. And Larry began a long career in real estate that eventually saw him go into income property and syndication—developing Motel 6 sites and some local commercial and housing developments.

He even edited a book, which was published in 1972—*Corporate Real Estate, Development and Management*. A few years later, he proudly gave a copy of the book to Cate School while son Michael was enrolled. Some thirty years then passed, and after the turn of the millennium, Megan Crandell, Michael's daughter, also attended Cate. The clever girl checked to see if Grandpa Larry's book was still in the school's library. To her delight, it was. And with a rare distinction. Of all the books in the library, *Corporate Real Estate, Development and Management* was one of the very few that had never been checked out. Upon hearing this from his granddaughter, Larry didn't bat an eye. Most of the students, he said in a matter-of-fact voice, were waiting for the movie version.

Back in the 1970s, the book proved a prelude to a series of real estate deals. Though Larry did well in this field, he was better known for his wit. In a way, he was an anti-salesman, letting the client convince himself or herself of the value of a property. However, he delivered his marketing slogan with great gusto:

"List with Crandell Realty, and you'll never have to move!"

Later on in that decade, Larry became the President of Vagabond Motor Hotels, and later still had a stint developing Del Taco fast-food stores. But one of his most successful ventures was with his son Michael. They began a software company in the mid 1980s. Their main product was a word processor called Sunword, which was designed by Michael. The company grew quickly and eventually served clients in six different countries. When an offer to buy the company was too good to pass up, they used the money from the sale to join forces again and create a new product that enabled people to send high quality computer-based faxes. This company was eventually acquired by a Silicon Valley technology firm that went public and became Efax—which is still very healthy today.

"It was a very profitable venture," Larry told the *News-Press* in a 2003 article. "But even more thrilling was getting to work with my son on the project."

Larry went on to become involved in a number of business adventures—including the founding of City Commerce Bank. But it is his approach to business rather than his *curriculum vitae* that stands out most to me.

Nothing sums up that approach better than the philosophy he taught me early in my life. The idea is straightforward: If you want people to have faith in you, you must start by having faith in yourself.

In the business world this idea often found expression in Larry's "work now, find out your salary later" strategy. Larry would go to someone who might hire him. He would offer to work for a week or two or even a month on spec, explaining that at the end of that time period he would be happy to accept whatever pay the employer thought was appropriate.

The approach is risky, for there is no guarantee how much pay one might receive. But I don't know of a single time it didn't work well for my dad. The strategy got his foot in the door and gave him the chance to show what he could do. He ended up landing some plum jobs, and he always started off with an employer by showing that he had confidence in himself.

Larry, being Larry, never abandons his sense of humor, no matter how serious the situation or project. One of my favorite business stories about him shows how he uses his wry wit to great effect.

Larry had been trying to get a well-known Santa Barbara developer to meet with him so that Larry could present a proposal. The developer was polite, but never agreed to a meeting.

After some time, Larry sent the developer a letter along with a $1,000 check. Larry wrote that he realized the developer's time was valuable—estimating it was worth about $2,000 per hour. Larry wrote further that he hoped the developer would accept the check for $1,000 to secure a half-hour meeting during his busy day.

Larry very quickly got a phone call and then an appointment with the developer. The developer was amused. He acknowledged that the check got his attention, but he told Larry flatly that he wasn't going to cash it. A few weeks later, Larry had signed up the same developer as a client.

The Encourager

"LARRY, thanks for the encouraging words today.... I have a sense you really understand my struggle here, and I needed your words today."

Those are the words of the executive director of a large Santa Barbara nonprofit. Its gifted leader had spent a very difficult two years at the helm of a charity that had been buffeted by a number of difficulties.

The executive director was stressed. His spirits were very low. At a meeting, Larry listened to the man's difficulties and launched into a speech of appreciation for all the man had done in the face of major obstacles. Larry then offered to join the charity's board.

The meeting finished with the executive director happy and energized. It was quite a transformation. I know because I was there. I wrote an e-mail to Larry afterwards:

> You are a father figure to him. You accept him and his feelings; you offer him admiration and respect; and most importantly, you express faith in his ability and his approach. He sees his experience as a "struggle." Your belief and understanding are a fillip which helps him to push onwards.
>
> I hereby dub you—"The Encourager."
>
> You rouse the dying embers of self-belief in people who are engaged in good work. They receive more than bonhomie and compassion. They gain strength.
>
> Love,
> Steven

Brittany, the Little Engine That Could

WE MET Larry on November 19, 1997, at the Goleta Teen of the Year awards ceremony. Our daughter, Brittany, was one of the finalists. The fact that she had been nominated was a surprise and a joy. We were smiles from ear to ear.

Our daughter had struggled very hard throughout her school career because of moderate to severe learning disabilities in all areas. Plus, a severe knee injury had meant she had to give up track, at which she had excelled and which brought joy to her heart. To us, her nomination seemed like a fairy-tale ending. Little did we know the fairy tale had just begun.

Larry was full of emotion as he introduced Brittany and she walked to the stage on her dad's arm. Larry then asked her to stand next to him on the stage as he finished. He gave her the best introduction of the evening by far. Those moments still bring tears of joy to my eyes and a warm glow to my heart. After the ceremony, Larry took Brittany and Tom (her dad) aside and talked with them for some time. I sat across the room in awe watching Mr. Larry Crandell, one of the most important men in our community, talking to my daughter and husband. What a wonderful night.

Larry then took the time to get to know us. We talked on the phone. We had a meeting in his office. We couldn't believe it and, boy, it was just what Brittany needed. Learning disabilities are very hard on self-esteem. The interest Larry took in Brittany changed her life in such a positive way. He actually changed all of our lives.

We were invited to lunch at Moby Dick. We arrived and were treated like royalty. There was an easel sign welcoming Brittany—all the way from Goleta! We had a wonderful time.

Then it was graduation time. Larry actually came to her graduation party. He didn't stay long, but he gave her a generous gift. He took the time to set up a meeting with Peter McDougall, the president of Santa Barbara City College (SBCC), because he felt Brittany needed to know him personally. Larry knew that SBCC was going to be rough for her, but he wanted to do everything he could to help.

Larry gave Brittany new hope, and her self-esteem rose. She was willing to go to more extensive tutoring, because she knew she could do it. And guess what? She did do it.

Brittany is now a mother and running her own day care business with a waiting list. We have the pleasure of seeing Larry each November at the Goleta Teen of the Year ceremony, and he always asks about her. They have such a special bond. She has always been the little engine that could, but when she was climbing that highest hill and starting to slip Larry was there to give her a much-needed push.

—*Sherri Miller*
Brittany's mother

All Talk, No Pay—The Nonprofit Emcee

LARRY owes his career as a master of ceremonies for nonprofit events in Santa Barbara to the fact that he was 40 years old and out of shape in 1963. Reading the newspaper one day, he discovered there was a physical fitness class run by the Santa Barbara Department of Parks and Recreation at Dwight Murphy Field near East Beach. It was called "Huff and Puff." Oddly enough, Larry's participation in the noontime touch football games there led to his career in community work.

It all started when Larry's friend Donnie Paulsen was retiring from his job with the parks and recreation department. Larry called a meeting of the Huffers and Puffers and said, "Why don't we do something for Donnie?" A simple program was produced on a folded piece of copy paper. More than 100 people were invited. Larry had his first Santa Barbara emcee job.

"It was a very low-budget thing," says Larry. "The food, as I recall, was 100 pounds of potato salad, served on paper plates at noon." But from the beginning, Larry showed his ability to recruit others to join a worthy effort. Larry's cast included Sam Battistone Jr., the head of Sambo's Restaurants, and Bill Bertka, who later went on to an NBA coaching career.

"I loved doing it. All the guys were jocks and their friends. It was very satisfying."

Larry soon started taking the microphone at YMCA fund-raisers. From there, one event literally led to another—as people would see him emcee for one charity and call him afterwards to help with another. Though Larry hasn't been counting, even a conservative estimate of the number of times he's emceed would be in the thousands. In his twenty years of presiding over Channel City Club luncheons, introducing some of the most distinguished speakers to come to Santa Barbara, Larry has emceed more than 500 events alone.

One reason for the large number of emcee jobs is that Larry has always been generous with his time. For decades, all people had to do to get Larry to help was ask.

"I'm working on six capital campaigns right now," Larry told the *News-Press* in 2003. "I'm not good at saying no. If I were a woman, I'd have a terrible reputation. My nickname is Mr. Ubiquitous, which I think is quite appropriate."

But speaking in public is never a sacrifice. "I've always welcomed the opportunity. I've often prepared more for my emceeing of charity events than I have for my business meetings."

Larry says the organization of an event is the key to its success, and things that others might find unimportant—like acoustics—are paramount to him because he knows that an audience who can't understand what's being said will lose interest quickly. An uninterested audience can hardly be expected to give generously.

"It's a gamble until the first roar of approval washes over you," says Larry.

That approval—whether it be applause or laughter—is manna to Larry. In 2005, at a Goleta Chamber of Commerce event called "Goleta's Finest," Larry was introduced as the co-emcee. There were 900 people in attendance filling the grand ballroom of the Bacara Resort. Larry tells the tale:

"As I walked toward the stage, I got a standing ovation. If you're 204 pounds, it's hard to be impish, but that's the way I felt. So I was extremely self-indulgent. I went to the mike and said, 'Folks I'm 82 years old. I'm really touched by this. I wonder if you would do me a favor. If I returned to my seat, would you do it again?' As I said it, I knew it would resonate. I returned to my seat, came back, and they redoubled their efforts. Which was what I was looking for. My fix."

Of course, the audience's response was due at least in part to the sense of gratitude Santa Barbarans feel after more than four decades of Larry's help with nonprofits. But they also enjoy his shenanigans. Who else would ask for a second helping of a standing ovation? His honesty about his appetite for acclaim—combined with his, yes, "impish" charm—here offered a humorous surprise during an event that, like many such worthy community events, was thoroughly predictable.

In the end, that is Larry's chief grace as an emcee. He allows people to "expect the unexpected." He might do anything. Audiences know that, and that's why they appreciate him so much.

Prominent Santa Barbara lawyer and long-time charity champion Joe Howell has a story that illustrates how Larry can use the element of surprise to electrify the proceedings.

Joe himself was emceeing the awards for a doctor/lawyer dinner at La Cumbre Country Club. Awards were being given out for tennis and golf competitions, and it was "really dragging out," according to Joe. So Larry, who was in the audience and a good friend of Joe's, came up on stage and whispered, "Would you like some help with the prizes?" Joe said sure. Larry said, "Okay, you read the awards and I'll give out the prizes." So Joe read the first name, "John Doe, for longest drive."

Larry took a full bottle of wine, which was the prize, and threw it across the room to the recipient. Fortunately, the man caught it.

The audience was suddenly very attentive. "People were saying, 'Oh my god, this could take out a doctor,'" said Joe.

Almost all the prizes were bottles of wine. But there were no injuries on that night, and boredom was replaced with oohs and ahs. What would have taken 25 minutes was reduced to four. And once the people in the audience got over their sense of impending disaster, they loved it.

At the end of the awards, Larry picked up a large vase with flowers and said, "That's it for the wine. Anyone else want a prize?"

The Auctioneer's Apprentice

ABOUT 20 years ago (I must have been a mere child, and Larry just a young buck of 63), I had the great fortune to cut my teeth as a charity auctioneer with the master himself. It was my first public attempt at draining money from people's pockets for a great cause, and Larry, who had long before written the book on that subject, showed me how it was done. Working in tandem with me, he guided me through that evening like a ballroom dance master.

In the years since, when our paths have been fortunate enough to cross, Larry often recounts that evening to those within earshot. In his usual comedic and self-deprecating style, Larry tells a version of that evening that has *him* hanging on to *my* coat tails, when of course the opposite was true. Larry, ever the trumpeter of other people's horns, showed me how to succeed and then made sure I felt that I did.

Larry is a fixture in the Santa Barbara community. We are so very fortunate to profit from his charm, wit and genuine caring. I am honored to have shared a microphone with him on one enchanted evening.

—*Layla Khashoggi*
Philanthropist and auctioneer extraordinaire

Family Reunited. Just back from the war in 1945, the Crandells met in Newark for this photo. From the left—Larry's brother Sam, his mother Jane, Larry, aged 22, and brother Marty, who was only 16 years old at the time of the photo. "Too young to fight overseas," says Larry about Marty, "but not too young to box. I challenged him to go a round—even though he was six years younger, he cleaned my clock." *Nota bene:* Larry holds his mother's hand in the portrait.

NIT 1946. Fresh from flying missions over Europe, Larry went straight into metaphorical battle as a starter for the Syracuse University basketball team. (Larry is far left in the bottom row.) This team qualified for the National Invitational Tournament—at the time more prestigious than the NCAA competition. Larry shot a two-hand set shot. (It was so long ago that there was nothing uncommon about shooting with two hands.) He remembers the thrill of playing at Madison Square Garden. For the record, the Orangemen were ousted in the first round by Muhlenberg 47–41. Photo courtesy of Syracuse University

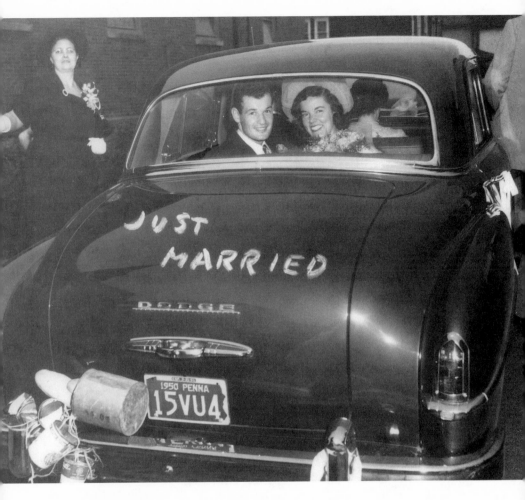

Journey's Beginning. Larry and Marcy were married in Marcy's hometown of Ashley, Pennsylvania on July 3, 1950. At left, Lena Novak, Marcy's mother prepares to farewell the couple. Five children, nine grandchildren, two great grandchildren and more than 55 years of marriage lay in front of the young couple.

The Potentially Endless Honeymoon. The newlyweds danced so well at their resort the management offered them free accommodation for as long as they wanted if they only did a 15-minute dance exhibition every night. They extended their stay for a week with the permission of their employer, Arthur Murray. Here, they dance at the outdoor nightclub at the Castle Harbour Hotel in Bermuda.

New Jersey Tan. "That's what I looked like at 180 pounds," says Larry. "It was in Bermuda. But I still had the Newark, New Jersey tan." By coincidence, these two Arthur Murray teachers also were in Bermuda for a vacation while Larry and Marcy honeymooned. Larry explains. "One did not go to Bermuda in July. *We* went to Bermuda in July. The other teachers were similarly not members of the cognoscenti."

Second Honeymoon. Larry and Marcy went back to Bermuda in 1958. They won an Arthur Murray competition called the Dancers Derby and used the money to take 21 staffers from the dance studio on a ship from Baltimore. "I don't remember the sweater," says the Silver Tongue. "You can see how much better looking your mother was for a woman than I was for a man."

Nice Threads. 1958, sailing for Bermuda. "Man, I liked myself in this one," says Larry. "Good hair. I don't remember the suit, though." But he does remember the trip. "There was a terrible storm. Marcy was the only one in the dining room. She ate heartily. I was coughing up my cookies. Because we booked 21 passages we had the owner's suite—that was big time. But when you're puking, one suite looks a lot like another."

Serious Business Circa 1960. The Arthur Murray world might have been glitz, glamour and gaiety, but Larry, age 37, decided a sober managerial image was best to project as he began his short reign as owner of the Santa Barbara studio. Larry's sartorial comment 46 years later: "Too much cuff shows." Photo by Dick Johnston, courtesy of the *Santa Barbara News-Press*

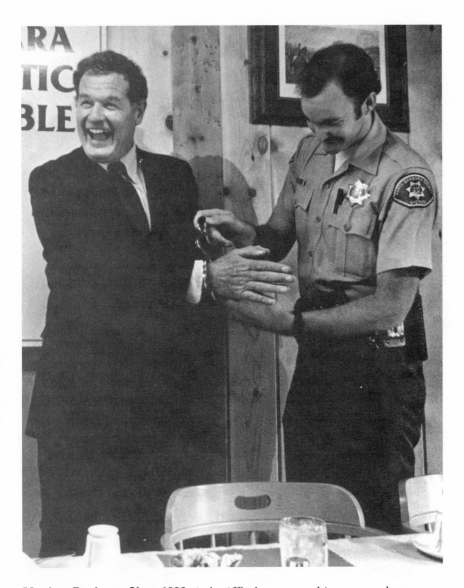

Monkey Business Circa 1986. A sheriff's deputy gets his man at a banquet at Earl Warren Showgrounds. But even the strong arm of the law can't take away Larry's sense of fun. It was a Santa Barbara Athletic Roundtable event. Santa Barbara City College basketball coach Frank Carbajal set up the ambush. The deputy interrupted proceedings and announced he was arresting Larry for shooting too much in pick-up basketball games. Larry pleaded guilty. It made the front page of the News-Press sports section. Photo by Bob Ponce, courtesy of the *Santa Barbara News-Press*

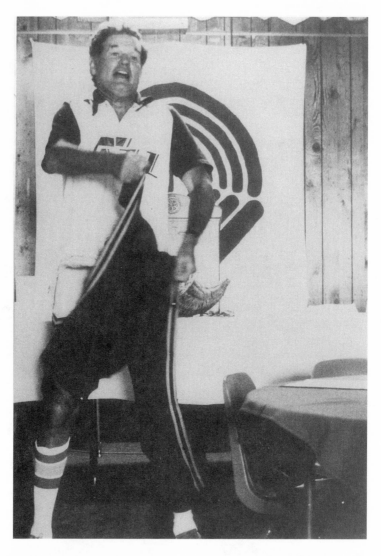

Strip-tease for Charity. The scene: a fund-raiser for the United Way at Santa Barbara's Cabrillo Arts Center. Larry offered to strip if enough money was raised. "Sam Battistone, co-owner of the Utah Jazz, had given me a complete authentic Jazz uniform," says Larry. "I didn't sleep in it, but I really loved wearing it." With two hundred people in the audience the fund-raising target was reached and Larry ripped off his pants to reveal his authentic NBA shorts. (For the record, Larry strenuously denies that someone offered to double the amount raised if he would only put his clothes back on—and quickly.)

Larry, Marcy and the President. Ronald Reagan spoke at the Santa Barbara Biltmore as a benefit for the Cancer Society. It took place after Reagan's second term as president. Larry can't remember the year, but he does remember a unique fund-raising idea. "Everyone who paid $500 got a photo with him. He was affability personified. I emceed the event. The Secret Service said I should introduce him as the 40th President, not the 'ex-' or 'former president' which was good advice because otherwise I would have made that mistake. I got goose pimples even though I disliked his actions as governor of California." Afterwards, Larry was asked if it was his first time introducing a president. "I did Woodrow Wilson," he said without batting an eyelash. "But there was a long gap between presidents." Larry then smiled. "The first time? What do you think? Oh yeah. It was a thrill."

Hello, Larry. The master emcee had the opportunity to introduce former Broadway star Carol Channing at a cocktail party before a benefit concert in 2005. Carol burst out laughing after hearing the Silver Tongue sing a few bars of her trademark song, "Hello Dolly." The benefit concert was called "An Evening with the Stars of the Greatest Generation." Actress and singer Rhonda Fleming also performed during the concert. When Larry introduced her, he asked how many great loves she had experienced. "Four," she answered. "Counting you, Larry."

Larry and Pat. No exact date on this photo, but judging from Larry's hair it's probably the late 1980s. Larry holds a basketball signed by the then world-champion Los Angeles Lakers. (You can just make out Magic Johnson's signature on the ball.) Larry is auctioning off the ball to benefit Westmont College. Former Lakers coach Pat Riley beams at the Silver Tongue banter. "I was really impressed with Pat and his family," says Larry. "Chris, his wife, is as pretty as he is handsome. They adopted two kids a year apart. I had to get a cottage for them and the two babies at the Biltmore. They were one of the most popular couples in the world at the time because of his success. And for free, he took the time to stop and speak for Westmont. The next day, a corporation paid him $10,000 for an hour speech. He did three or four benefits for Westmont or Santa Barbara City College. One of them was at (the architect) Barry Berkus' house. A bunch of us had paid to go through a 'basketball clinic' with the master coach. He said he was going to run through a typical Lakers practice. He then threw out the balls and walked away. When we stopped laughing, he set up some plays. He told me I would take the part of Kurt Rambis. I allowed as I would rather be James Worthy (a more glamorous and talented player). 'So would Rambis,' said the coach."

Larry, Software Wizard. July, 1986. Son Michael sits at the keyboard in their Coast Village Road office—now the site of the Montecito gelato shop, Scoop. Larry helped Michael get started in the software business—putting up the initial financing. A company, and a partnership, was born. One of Larry's favorite stories is the day he marched into Michael's office and discovered a key fact about the I.T. revolution. "I was really pissed off," says Larry. "Not about the company. We were doing fine and Michael's performance was excellent. For me, it was an issue of fairness. By that time, we had grown to have about 20 employees. Every one of them had e-mail, but I didn't. I told Michael I wasn't going to stand for it anymore. He said 'Dad, you need to get a computer first.'" Photo by Steve Malone courtesy of the *Santa Barbara News-Press*

Silver Tongue Symphony. An estimated 7,000 people crammed into the sunken gardens by the Santa Barbara County Courthouse for the July 4 free Pops concert in 2000. The guest conductor that day wore his trademark bowtie. Though his musical talents qualified him to conduct a piece with the complexity of, say, "Row, Row, Row Your Boat," he bravely took the baton to lead the Santa Barbara Symphony in a John Philip Sousa march. Before the song, Larry cornered a young cellist and told her that though it was just one song, he wanted her to give it every ounce of feeling she had. Not knowing his penchant for seemingly serious self-mockery, she looked at him as if he were a candidate for sedative medication. Larry reports the young cellist recovered from the shock and played magnificently. Photo ©Joanne A. Calitri International.

Congressman Huffington. Larry's 70th birthday in 1993 was the excuse for a very successful fund-raising event. Michael Huffington, member of the U.S. House of Representatives for the 22nd District which included Santa Barbara County, joined with his wife Arianna to throw an extravagant benefit dinner in Larry's honor. "Michael was gracious and generous to charities. In 1994, he launched his campaign for U.S. senator at another multi-millionaire's house. Fifty very wealthy people were listening to him speak. I was sitting with Arianna and I whispered that it was a new campaign, but the same old sports jacket. She made him stop speaking and then told everyone what I had said. Michael smiled. He loved anything that made him look like the common man. By the way, the 'old' sports coat was a $1500 Baroni." Huffington went on to spend $28 million of his personal fortune on the Senate campaign, but lost the race to Dianne Feinstein by 1.6 percent of the vote. (Larry's children, Leslie, Larry, Jr. and Michael Crandell, are in the background to the left.)

Viva La Fiesta. "This was during my fat period," says Larry. Dressed for Santa Barbara's Old Spanish Days celebration in August, Larry and Marcy pose in clothes tailored just for the event. "Marcy bought a suit for $1.50 at the thrift store and cut it into a bolero type. Then she made the ample cummerbund." Larry and Marcy were well-known for their ballroom dancing displays at the Coral Casino during Fiesta.

As You've Never Seen Him Before. Larry and Marcy reversed their normal roles for this charity bash. "Beauty and the Beast" was the theme. Larry sports a pert and pretty wig with a dress that reveals plenty of shoulder while remaining modest when it comes to his décolletage. He swears his nail polish matched his lipstick perfectly.

Olympic Run. The 1996 Olympic Torch Relay made its way through Santa Barbara on an 84-day, 15,000-mile journey across the United States. Though Larry was short-of-breath as he ran—he would have open-heart surgery in 1998—he regards bearing the torch as one of his fondest memories. The torch bearers pictured here: (bottom row, from left) Sal Rodriguez, Larry, Al Pizano; (top row, from left) Jack Bianchi, Gerd Jordano, Jeff Farrell and Peter MacDougall.

He Ain't Heavy. At the Coral Casino, in 1997, Larry's 74th birthday also became a fund-raiser. Steven was living in New Zealand at the time and flew out to surprise Larry. But Larry was ready with a surprise of his own. He jumped into Steven's arms. Steven's son Luke, aged 4 at the time, seemed to be considering what would happen if he had to catch Grandpa Larry. "He'd have been squashed," says Grandpa. "I certainly didn't plan the leap," Larry adds. "Steven came across the room, and I decided to take a risk. I was just trying to keep a light touch to what was an emotional time." Though tempted, Steven did not drop his father. Photo courtesy of the *Santa Barbara News-Press*

Larry, Rocky & the
Santa Barbara Symphony

WHEN virtuoso guitarist Angel Romero agreed to conduct the Santa Barbara Symphony for its annual July 4th concert in 2005 at the county court house, Larry Crandell volunteered to introduce him to the 6,000-plus persons gathered on the sunny lawn.

Larry did a great job of whipping the audience into a frenzy to welcome the maestro. And for the first half of the concert Larry waited quietly in the wings, planning his next entrance.

Then, when the maestro started the orchestra in a rousing rendition of Bill Conti, Jr.'s "Theme from *Rocky*," Larry donned a grey hooded sweatshirt and went down in front of the stage. As the music rose towards its climax, Larry bounded up the stairs and pumped his fists energetically into the air, shadow-boxing impressively with an imaginary Apollo Creed.

At 82 years of age, he was a sight to behold. The crowd went nuts. It was a great moment for the Santa Barbara Symphony. Thanks, Larry, for making everyone smile.

—John Robinson
Executive director, Santa Barbara Symphony

The Heart Attack, or How to Have Fun While Confronting Mortality

MANY PEOPLE have the ability to look right past the silver lining and find the dark cloud at the heart of human experience. But not many can stare at the dark cloud and see that it, too, holds richness, meaning and sometimes joy.

Larry is far from being a Pollyanna—he prides himself on his ability to analyze things critically and see them for what they are. But, as you know, he also wields the potent tool of appreciation which, combined with his sense of playfulness, can turn even a life-threatening event into a bit of a romp.

So it was with his heart attack. It happened on March 17, 1985, after a game of basketball. He was playing on what he called an "old men's" team. Most of the players were over 40; Larry himself was almost 62.

"As luck would have it," Larry told me about a year after the event, "I shot about as well as I am capable of shooting. I really had a great day. But during the contest, I began to feel as if I had a cold or the flu. By the time I finished, I felt really lousy.

"I'm a great believer that a good night's sleep will cure anything—including leprosy. I was disappointed when I rose the next morning only to feel empty and tired."

He went to see his G.P., Dr. Tony Allina, who gave him some tests. A short time later, Marcy drove him to the cardiac care unit at Santa Barbara Cottage Hospital. It was the first time he had stayed overnight in a hospital since 1944 in Italy. But Larry wasn't worried.

"Something about being in the hospital is very comforting to me. Some people hate it. I think: Hey, if anything else goes wrong, I've got the best care right here. So I clowned around a lot. They hooked me up to take my pulse, and I'd bounce on the bed and knock the pulse up. I think the highest I got was 107."

At least the doctors were serious. An electrocardiogram followed by an angiogram revealed he had suffered a heart attack. Larry used a driving analogy to describe his condition to the *News-Press* less than two months later.

"They determined that I had a vessel in the back of my heart clogged, and that was causing the discomfort and the heart attack. And they found that one of the three main arteries was 40 percent occluded. The tests also showed that my heart had collateral vessels.... I envision it sort of like Highway 101 being temporarily closed for repairs and using Coast Village Road."

Larry felt a "great oxygen debt" when they tested him on the treadmill, but did not feel much pain. In fact, when word got out about the heart attack, the experience became rather pleasurable. Phone calls, letters and postcards started arriving. Not to mention people. "The visits were wonderful and upbeat," remembers Larry. "I felt cared about. In fact, I had a very good time in the hospital.

"One of the things a nurse said which I enjoyed very much was— 'Larry, you are the healthiest-looking person we've ever had here at the cardiac care unit.' I told her to be the healthiest in this environment is like being the tallest midget."

After a week in the hospital, Larry came home. After three more weeks, Larry returned to his emceeing duties at a Santa Barbara Athletic Roundtable luncheon. "For the first time, the salutation 'How are you?' became a real question," Larry says. The luncheon went well, and Larry's good health returned. But his brush with mortality had made a profound impact on his life.

He vowed to change lifelong eating habits and went on the then-popular Pritikin diet. It was not Larry's dream cuisine. "We get the best food money can buy, throw it away, and eat the cartons it comes in," he said.

He also decided to set a goal for himself. A good friend, George Smanez, who was then 84 himself, confronted Larry one day. "He came up to me and slapped me," Larry remembers. "Lovingly, though. The guy was about 5'3". He told me: 'How long do you plan to live?' I said I thought I'd live forever like most people, until they get sick."

George was adamant. He insisted that Larry come up with a plan. "So I said, 'Okay, George. I'm 62. I'm going to live till I'm 82.

Twenty years.' He said, 'Okay, what are your goals?' I said, 'Well, just moving along, enjoying each day as it comes. Try to have some fun each day.' "

It wasn't good enough for George. So Larry started thinking about it and decided there was one goal at the top of his list—to become master of ceremonies and president of one of the most distinguished clubs in town, the Channel City Club.

It had been founded in 1946 by one of the most civic-minded Santa Barbarans of the 20th century, Louie Lancaster. Louie was one of the three men who founded Santa Barbara Bank and Trust. He was also a gifted speaker, a leading philanthropist and known as…you guessed it…Mr. Santa Barbara.

At the time of Larry's heart attack, Louie was 90 and still emceeing for the Channel City Club. The club had a membership of more than a thousand local people and a reputation for bringing nationally known leaders to speak in Santa Barbara. (It still does, having celebrated its 60th anniversary in 2006.)

Larry had an enormous amount of respect for Louie, but until the heart attack Larry hadn't really thought about taking on such a regular responsibility.

Louie, however, *had* been thinking about it. "Louie said he'd like to groom me as his replacement," remembers Larry. "Unfortunately, the last five guys he groomed had all died."

In 1986, about a year after his heart attack, and despite the curse of being Louie's chosen one, Larry fulfilled his goal to become the emcee of the bi-weekly luncheons.

He's now been doing it for more than 20 years. Over the years he's created a great rapport with the members and with the distinguished speakers—people as diverse as former California governor Pete Wilson; Senator Barbara Boxer; Donald Regan, former White House chief of staff to Ronald Reagan; James Nordstrom, the co-chairman of the department store chain; Marilyn Horne, the opera star; Julia Child, the chef and author; and a number of Nobel laureates.

"After more than 500 luncheons," says Larry, " I still look forward to them—and to interacting with friends in the audience—with the same amount of joy I did in the beginning."

The Channel City Club was only part of the happy ending to the heart attack—a happy ending that's been unfolding for more than two decades. Larry's career as a community leader has grown substantially since the day in 1985 when he checked into the cardiac care unit. Most people hardly remember the heart attack. Larry does. The memory is a daily reminder to live well.

"Anyone who's been startled into recognizing his own mortality begins to think in terms of—Will I enjoy today? You need to work at keeping your life lively. If the journey isn't all, it's a bad investment."

Special Intelligence

I MET Larry soon after moving to Santa Barbara in 1992. The rather exciting topic of satellite reconnaissance had just been declassified by President Clinton and I was recruited to give a talk about it to the Channel City Club. Larry introduced me with his marvelous wit, and I knew immediately that I would like to get to know him better. That was easier than I expected. I was soon asked to join the governing group of the Channel City Club on which he also served.

This gave us a chance to worry together about an ancient and important institution here in Santa Barbara. The Channel City Club is a precarious enterprise, operating as it does without a proper endowment. Its only capital is the enthusiastic support of a large and active membership. Larry recognized that we needed to create a modest reserve for its operations. He suggested that we establish special memberships for those who were able to give extra support to such organizations. Thus were born the Century and Lancaster Club memberships. It was a daring move, but it has underwritten the health and vitality of the organization ever since. It is very much to his credit that the Channel City Club continues to provide a Window on the World for Santa Barbara.

—Dr. Albert D. Wheelon
Former deputy director of the CIA and
satellite reconnaissance pioneer

Joy, Basketball & Blood Pressure

I PLAYED basketball with Larry at Barry Berkus' house in Hope Ranch for years. [Barry is a noted local architect and basketball fanatic.] Larry finally retired from the game (as I recently have), but I will always remember two things. One big and one small.

The big one was that Larry always brought joy to the game. He disapproved of any arguing. If there was some heated disagreement among the other players (myself included), Larry could always defuse the situation with a joke or a look that made the aggressors feel foolish. His intervention would soon get us back on track for our friendly Sunday morning game.

The small one was that Larry had probably the last two-handed set shot I ever witnessed on a court, and it usually went in. I knew he was a great competitor when he returned to playing *after* his heart attack, asking Dr. Tony Allina, his G.P. and fellow basketballer, to check his blood pressure between games.

I consider Larry my friend, but then again, I think everyone who comes in contact with Larry thinks of him as a friend.

—*Marv Bauer*
Attorney

Shoulder to Shoulder
with a World Champion Coach

This story appeared in the Santa Barbara News-Press *in 1993. It shows how Larry's love of sport, his charity work and his sense of humor all work together. Reporter Ben Hellwarth tells the tale.*

❦

WHEN it comes to raising money for others, Larry Crandell says he has no qualms about putting on an act.

When former Los Angeles Lakers' basketball coach Pat Riley [who won the 2006 NBA title with the Miami Heat] came to a Westmont College fund-raising auction, he brought the game board showing the strategy he sketched for Magic Johnson to score the basket that ensured one of the Lakers' championships.

Crandell remembers telling Riley that he might only get $100 for it. Riley thought it was worth more. So did Crandell. The emcee cooked up a little game plan of his own.

He told Riley: "If you're willing to have me really insult you, and wake up the audience, we can get a lot more than that."

With Riley's permission, Crandell got the ball rolling.

"Everybody knows Riley," Crandell recalled saying. "He's movie-star handsome, he's a great dresser, he's a great coach. But I want to introduce you to him as the world's worst auctioneer."

Crandell then "played the heavy," relying on his reputation as the ultimate auctioneer, the veteran pitchman who was going to trounce the novice Riley right before the audience's eyes in a lopsided contest to see who could raise more for the same game board—and therefore for Westmont.

The plot worked.

"The audience hears this hero being picked on. So Riley got up and he doesn't know how to do it, but it didn't matter. People fell over themselves. We got 800 bucks."

Then came Crandell's turn. The bidding started at $5. Auctioneer Crandell eventually got the bids up to $350, "but they wanted to show me that he was more than twice as good."

Crandell wound up as the butt of his own joke—intentionally. Self-deprecation is one of Crandell's favorite comic tools. He finds it a small price to pay.

—Ben Hellwarth
Santa Barbara News-Press

Participating Is the Only Thing

ONE THING should be obvious from this book: sports are central to Larry's life and to his philosophy of life. Larry always reveled in the games he played—whether it was touch football, basketball, ping-pong or tennis. The Newark kid who was picked last in the school-yard learned a lesson along the way. It's not about whether you win or lose, or even how well you play, it's about getting the chance to play at all.

In 1985, right after his heart attack, he articulated his feelings to John Zant of the *News-Press*.

"I abhor the 'winning isn't everything, it's the only thing' outlook. I think participating is the only thing.

"The camaraderie has meant as much as the game. I think you can get to know a guy better in three or four weeks of playing ball with him than you can in five years of going to church with him or doing business with him. The mock insult—'Hell, you were wide open on that lay-up, Larry. I thought for a minute you were going to dunk it.' A son saying, 'Dad, when you jump, you tuck your legs up, but your head stays in the same spot.' Being part of that. That's how I learned to love sports."

Anyone who participates can take part in the camaraderie. In that sense, sports are very democratic. Perhaps that is why Larry feels so motivated to help charities that help people get the chance to partici-pate—not just in sports, but in all endeavors.

Beyond camaraderie, there is another benefit to Larry's approach. If you prize participation above all, then it's hard to be a sore loser. Any time Larry got to play basketball, he counted himself a winner. He felt blessed just to be part of the game.

Indeed, he feels blessed to be part of life. That is perhaps one of his most powerful secrets.

Special Understanding

PEOPLE know Larry Crandell as a great communicator and a great humorist, but they sometimes miss the fact that he has the gift of compassionate understanding.

He once told an audience that for a special athlete from Santa Barbara to be able to travel to Los Angeles to compete is like you or me going to Switzerland to compete in the real Olympics.

He's right. Road trips for Special Olympics athletes are often the only vacations that they will be able to take. This travel is very, very important to them.

Larry understands that intuitively—which is probably why he is so effective at helping raise money for our cause.

—*Ada Conner*
Santa Barbara area director, Special Olympics

How to Be a Good Parent to a Young Athlete

Larry prides himself on his ability to immerse himself in the moment ("the journey is all") while at the same time being able to analyze and appreciate the events of his life with detachment. The balance between emotional involvement and rational distance is a challenging one to achieve. But to Larry, a father and athlete, it's important. Here are some excerpts from an article he wrote for a Goleta Valley South Little League publication in 1987:

ENCOURAGE your young athlete to participate. Comfort her when things go badly, and praise her when things go well.

Try not to criticize immediately after a game or a mistake. As a matter of fact, try to resist coaching your child at all, unless she asks for help. Instead, ask questions. Find out how your athlete feels about her performance.

Resist telling him how great you were. Youngsters tend to be in the hero worship stage up to ten years old. By the time he's 12 or so, he can observe your red face, your labored breath, your expanding waistline. Tell him of some of your defeats, your embarrassing moments. As he grows up, he'll think more of you for it, not less.

Throw away the rose-colored glasses and the selective memory. Were you perfect? Do you remember some of the "sins" you committed in your youth? Be fair—isn't your youngster ahead of you in some ways?

Try not to live your life vicariously through your child. You've had your chance. Don't resent his missing a shot, failing to go for a rebound. Forgive her if she's lax in defense. She doesn't need condemnation.

Your child shouldn't be used as an excuse for venting your frustrations over life's disappointments.

Chances are the coach is trying very hard, and earns many times over the small pittance the school or club pays him. Recognize that the coach will be on the job next year, and the year after, and the year after that. Your interest will plummet the day after your child graduates. The team support you provide is valuable and useful, albeit short-term. Keep it positive or say nothing.

Remember your lack of objectivity in evaluating your child's performance. You love him and cannot see him as others do. Try to control your emotional involvement. It's usually your own ego at work—not your love for your child. One of the most unattractive sights at a school or club sporting event is that of an irate parent screaming at an official, the coach or even one of the players.

The levels of competition from second grade through high school naturally become more difficult. The opportunities are available to fewer and fewer youngsters. Enjoy the experience *now*. Few of us become Boston Celtics.

It's easy to be proud and affectionate when your offspring has scored the key goal. The accolades then are sweet and good. But when the child has performed poorly, that's when the real "All-American" parent reminds the youngster of how much he or she is loved and how rich an experience it is to be his or her parent.

Remember [former] USC coach John McKay's dictum when Notre Dame's football team defeated the Trojans soundly: "Over one-half billion Chinese don't even know we played today!"

Eating Makes Me Hungry, or How to Get Diabetes Without Really Trying

LARRY'S brother Marty would get annoyed with Larry when it came to the subject of eating. Marty, who you'll remember won the NCAA heavyweight boxing title, was a splendid athlete and a hard worker. But he didn't have a lot of willpower when tempted by his older brother. Larry would bring out the junk food and start eating in front of Marty—offering to share his stash of sugar and fat. Marty would get irritated even as he began to indulge.

"Why do you do it, Lawrence?" the younger brother would say. "Even *you* feel lousy when you eat it."

"I know," said Larry. "But how great it feels sliding down."

Throughout his life, Larry used his cleverness to turn his terrible eating habits into part of his comedy act. He often talked about the book he was going to write called *Eating Makes Me Hungry*. Or he would expound on his theory of culinary arts which stated that if one sugary confection was good, then more must be better.

When he was a kid, he could sometimes get away with eating potato chips for dinner. In a poor household led by a lenient mother, the nutritional guidance was as limited as the variety of food in the house. When he was an adult, he maintained his childlike interest in junk food, sometimes putting away two large Snickers bars an hour before dinner. As a result, he reports he spent most of his adult life 20 to 25 pounds overweight.

In 1974, Larry commuted to San Diego for the work week. He was president of Vagabond Motor Hotels, and rather than move the family when he got the big job, he moved himself and came home for weekends.

Each Sunday evening, before he left for the 200-mile drive south, he would fortify himself by eating a quart of ice cream. Then, near Anaheim, about two hours into the journey, he would stop and pick up a six-pack of doughnuts. "I'd be groaning," Larry remembers, "but

I'd eat them. Ones with icing and sprinkles, raised glazed, French twists. The only kind I wouldn't eat was plain."

Larry has a clever-sounding explanation for his eating behavior. "I'm better at abstinence than moderation," he says. It's another one of his classic lines. But it leaves out the key point: He may be better at abstinence, but he's best at indulgence.

The habits of a lifetime proved hard to change even in the wake of the heart attack. Larry fell off the Pritikin wagon not too long after he climbed aboard. He resumed the snack-food binging that had driven his brother to despair decades earlier. Though "comfort food" is a phrase that wasn't in vogue for much of Larry's life, it fits his diet perfectly. Like Oscar Wilde, Larry could resist anything but temptation.

"Ice cream is still the sweetest-tasting thing," says Larry with a wistful look in his eye.

Larry gave up basketball in the late 1980s but continued to walk and jog and swim. Then came one of the greatest moments in his life—being selected by Santa Barbara County as one of seven "local heroes" to bear the Olympic torch as the relay passed through Santa Barbara on its way to Atlanta in 1996.

To say he was thrilled with the chance to carry the Olympic flame is an understatement. He immediately decided to start a training regime—going down to La Playa Stadium at Santa Barbara City College to work out. But no matter how often he tried to pick up the pace in his training, he simply could not manage it. His oxygen debt was a loan that could not be paid in full. "I could never get past the walk-and-jog stage." On May 2, he ran down Milpas Street—from Figueroa to Cota Streets—approximately a quarter mile, and all downhill. Crowds lined the street. People cheered, and Larry felt on top of the world—except for one thing. His breathing was very, very labored.

"As I ran I had two thoughts. One was the importance of carrying a torch that at the time was 100 years old—the same age as the modern Olympic movement itself. The second one was that if I wasn't sucking wind I would have enjoyed it more."

It sounds like a joke, but Larry was worried about finishing without expiring. "There was a guy at Marathon, Greece, who tried a longer race, as I recall," Larry says. "The end of the race also happened to be the end of him. I only went 400 meters. It was thrilling, but there was this little fear that maybe I wouldn't make it."

Two and a half years later, in August 1998, the reason for his shortness of breath became clear. A routine exam lead to the discovery that additional arteries had become occluded since his heart attack. He was immediately scheduled for a bypass operation.

"They billed me for a 6-way bypass," remembers Larry. "There's some question as to whether you can have that many without bringing in a partner."

Larry's convalescence was supposed to take six weeks. Instead, it took three or four months. Thirteen years after his heart attack, the experience was an arduous one.

He coped with equal amounts of humor and what he calls "self-delusion."

"There are two kinds of people in the world," says Larry. "Those who exaggerate maladies and those who try to minimize them. If I can keep myself jolly, I can avoid any sense of panic. So that's what I did."

In the end, Larry's approach, aided by some splendid nursing from Marcy, helped him recover remarkably well. So well that in June the next year, he joined myself and my brother Michael, Joe Howell, and *Santa Barbara News-Press* publisher Steve Ainsley on a road trip to San Francisco. Michael, Joe and Steve were competing in the Escape from Alcatraz triathlon. Larry and I were along to offer support and have some fun.

But Larry was still eating poorly. Picture an ice cream bar, a hot dog, and some pretzels—and all that was before we got to Paso Robles. He became extremely tired and dizzy.

When Larry returned, he happened to be raising money for the Sansum Diabetes Research Institute. The director there, nationally known researcher and specialist Dr. Lois Jovanovic, took his blood glucose count and, to quote Larry's very technical analysis, it was "way, way up." She diagnosed him as having type-II diabetes.

Larry immediately went on a modified version of the Atkins diet, drastically limiting the amount of carbohydrates he ate. He also took medication and began testing his own blood glucose every day, as do millions of other diabetics in America.

In what Larry describes as "quite a victory," his system made a comeback. After a number of months, Dr. Jovanovic told him his pancreas was functioning at 80 percent. She said that if Larry stuck to his diet and continued with his exercise he could control the disease without medication.

But what could not be undone was the damage his diabetic and pre-diabetic condition probably did to his heart. Diabetes and heart disease go hand in hand—diabetics are twice as likely to have heart attacks. All of Larry's clever words can't change the fact that his poor diet put his health at risk.

"I get an ulcer when I think of taking care of the guy," says Larry's physician at the Veteran's Administration, Dr. Joe Blum. "Larry is the greatest treasure this town has. When I see him at the dais of all the charity benefits, and when I think of all the money he's raised for good causes, I just start worrying—am I doing everything I can for him? I just want to keep Larry going as long as possible."

Most of the time, the Silver Tongue does his part to stay healthy. He lays off the carbs and tests his blood daily. His diabetes is still under control, and he weighs in at a trim 204 pounds.

What It's Like to Be Larry Crandell

Larry has confessed to me that he often sees himself as both actor and director in the movie of his life. Here he takes on the role of author as well, telling an anecdote about himself.

∾

IN 1996, after the Olympic torch bearers finished their segments, we were picked up by a car and taken to bleachers that had been set up adjacent to the Santa Barbara railway station.

There, a crowd gathered. The size was estimated at less than 40,000, but more than 200.

Each of the seven of us torch bearers was given a chance to speak. Mike Takeuchi, who worked at the time at the Mental Health Assessment House, got up to speak. He had to wait as the sustained applause died down.

"Now I know," he said, "even if it's just for a moment, what it's like to be Larry Crandell."

I must admit I found the words most pleasing—mostly for what they say about what I have received in my life. As a youngster, I never would have imagined in my wildest dreams that my fate in life would be to receive applause or honors of any kind. I have been truly blessed. Thank you, Mike, for your kind words. I have enjoyed every minute.

—*Larry Crandell*
Olympic torch bearer

What All Charities Should Know

SANTA Barbara County has an estimated 1,500 nonprofits—that's more than one for every 300 residents. One recent study said the area had not only the most charities per capita in Southern California, but also the most generous populace. Experts say the level of giving is so high that few regions in the entire country rival it.

By any measure, Larry Crandell's home is a hotbed of eleemosynary activity. And if you were to ask anyone in the nonprofit field to name one of the most prominent fund-raisers and volunteers, one of the leading philanthropic activists and strategists and perhaps the single person most associated with charitable giving in the community, the answer would be Larry Crandell.

So when Larry talks about what makes people volunteer for and give to charities, people listen. Even if Larry proposes a paradox.

Consider this statement:

"If you want people to like you, have them do a favor for you."

One of Larry's first moves when he begins to help a charity is to find out what kind of volunteer support it has—from its board and from the community. If the charity is new, he looks to how volunteer support can be developed.

How does he do this?

He follows his own advice, naturally. He devises ways that people can do favors for the charity and have the wonderful feeling of helping a worthy cause. In essence, Larry builds relationships by inspiring the goodwill of others.

Here's an example. The Teddy Bear Foundation was a brand new charity in 2003. Its purpose is to help the families of children with cancer cope with their added financial burdens. With money worries eased, the parents can then focus on loving their ill child, who is often undergoing invasive treatment. The charity was a great idea, serving a need in the community. But it had no public profile and no volunteer or donor support. So Larry, Santa Barbara Chamber of Commerce Director Steve Cushman, and the charity's executive director, Nikki Simon, came up with a concept. They called it the Grizzly Club. They got on the phone and invited a number of local business leaders to breakfast to learn about how they could help—in other words, how they could do a favor for the new organization. The business leaders came, and over omelettes and coffee, they listened to the stories of families who were currently being helped by the foundation. All the business leaders became Grizzlies by volunteering their time or donating money.

Once these businessmen had volunteered and/or given (done the favor), they were involved. They were Grizzlies now. They had their own relationship with the new charity and the people it helped. The next year the pack of Grizzlies grew—the existing members recruiting others. People who were strangers to the charity became keen supporters.

Why? First, because of the charitable work Teddy Bear does, but also because the volunteers really like the charity. And why do they like it? Well, in the beginning, it was because they had done the charity a favor.

There is nothing like being needed to inspire loyalty. Ask any mother or father.

The Best Unpaid Employee

THE FIRST time I met Larry will always be a special memory. When I set up the Hutton Foundation, I realized that Larry was a force within the nonprofit community and that our relationship with each other could be important to the effectiveness of the foundation.

I was told that Larry had a verbal gift and liked to use it. Knowing that friendship between us could add to our ability to make a difference in the nonprofit sector, I let him know at our first meeting that for the two of us to work together, I would have to speak 50 percent of the time whenever we met.

He has worked hard to honor that commitment. I can only imagine how hard it's been, but it has made for a great friendship.

Larry is the greatest non-paid employee the Hutton Foundation has.

—Tom Parker
President, the Hutton Foundation

The Astronomical Sum of $250 Million

THE ONLY time I ever saw Larry embarrassed was at a planning committee luncheon for an upcoming Santa Barbara Youth Sports Association gala fund-raiser. It was in the mid-1990s, and it happened in front of a very high-powered committee—including big-time S.B. movers and shakers, such as Sheriff Jim Thomas, former CEO of Star Communications Chris Edgecomb and philanthropist Leslie Ridley-Tree.

Another well-known and much-revered member of this committee was Eva Haller, who by most folks' assessment, is another earth-mover when it comes to assisting charities. We were trying to figure out which citizen to honor, and Eva quietly got up from her chair and started reeling off facts and figures that embarrassed and at the same time amazed Larry—two very difficult things to do.

Eva had gone to the library and spent hours researching the local news and any other source she could get her hands on, and was able to ascertain that Mr. Charity, Larry Crandell, had worked on hundreds of charity events and fund-raising activities. And, most important, she discovered that he had helped raise the astronomical sum of $250 million for local services.

I remember the silence in the room after she stated this, followed by Larry's response. He said Eva was a little off, and that it was probably less than the number she'd mentioned—in fact, only about $200 million. We all laughed, but we had our honoree, and that year we raised a great deal of money in Larry's honor. It kept the Page Youth Center in business with a lot more programs and a lot happier staff. Of course, the kids who use the center were happiest of all.

It was only fitting, as Larry had helped raise money to build the center in the first place.

—Pat Steele
Executive vice-president, Starbuck, Tisdale & Associates

The Five Fundraising Senses

RAISING money is an art. Larry's approach is not to have a grand plan. Instead, he has what could be called an extemporaneous strategy. He starts with an idea, and then he begins to interact with the people he will need to make it work. The idea changes as he responds to the realities—and the personalities—of the particular situation.

But Larry is not sailing without a compass. He finds his way by regularly taking readings from his environment and by always keeping his senses about him.

Here are the five fundraising senses, according to Larry:

Sense of purpose: He never loses sight of what the nonprofit and the community is trying to achieve. He is flexible when it comes to strategy and technique, but he sticks to the goal with determination.

Sense of perspective: He always tries to see things from another's point of view. This helps him identify blind spots and anticipate problems.

Sense of joy: He wants to savor life and have a good time whenever possible. No meeting is so important that life's pleasures should be denied. No cause is so serious that Larry loses his sense of playfulness. Larry enjoys the journey, and he hopes to make the journey more enjoyable for his colleagues.

Sense of self: Larry is eager to add to his self-knowledge. Even the knowledge of his own limitations can act as a springboard for action. If he knows he *can't* do a job, he finds someone who's able to get it done. If he knows he *can* do it, he steps to the fore with confidence.

Sense of humor: This is the most important sense of all. Laughter is at the heart of Larry's stealth fundraising strategy. He uses it to put people at ease and to connect with them. In fact, humor is at the heart of pretty much everything Larry does.

Those are the master fund-raiser's five senses. The key to using them well, Larry will tell you, is awareness. You might think that, at 83, Larry misses a lot of what goes on. Nothing could be further from the truth. He is both observant and perceptive. He also has a habit of using the intelligence he gathers in a completely utilitarian manner—as long as it increases the coffers of charity.

When Friendship Becomes Unaffordable

Larry received this letter from his basketball buddy, Stan Hatch. It was sent on the letterhead of the legal firm Hatch & Parent. Larry says it is one of the funniest pieces of mail he's ever received.

∾

NOVEMBER 12, 1985

Dear Mr. Crandell,

During the past week I have received no less than five letters from as many charities all signed by you with the salutation "Dear Friend." In each instance you asked me, as your friend, to provide substantial financial support to the charity in question. After consultation with my accountant, I find that I can no longer afford to be your friend and would ask that you downgrade our relationship to "casual acquaintance."

Gratefully,

—*Stanley C. Hatch*

Three in One

IN THE 1980s, [Santa Barbara radio station] KDB was involved with numerous fund-raising promotions and parties for the Council of Christmas Cheer [now The Unity Shoppe]. At that time the organization, which was founded in 1936 to help the needy and cheer the sick and elderly, and which continues to help thousands of local families, was operating out of the Catholic Charities warehouse on Haley Street and open for distributions only for a few weeks during the holiday season.

One day in 1988, Council of Christmas Cheer director Barbara Tellefson came to my office and tearfully told me that a new location had to be found immediately for her organization. She was especially interested in the Victoria Street Theater building. Could I help? No. But maybe I knew someone who could. I phoned my friend (everybody's friend) Larry Crandell. In effect, he said, "Leave it to me."

A few days later, a meeting of Santa Barbara's leading citizens occurred at the Hope Ranch home of real estate investor Steve Lyons. Larry helped arrange finance and organized community support for the effort. With help from singer Kenny Loggins and many others, the project took shape. In the end, *three* local charities—The Council of Christmas Cheer (Unity Shoppe), Child Abuse Listening and Mediation (CALM) and the Retired Senior Volunteer Program (RSVP)—were able to acquire the Victoria Street Theater together. Eighteen years later, the three charities still share the building.

I always think of it as "The Larry Crandell Building."

—*Bob Scott*
Former owner, KDB radio

To Understand the Person, Understand the Dream

"DON'T just appreciate people for who they are—appreciate who they are trying to be." This is one of Larry's fundamental operating principles.

Larry knows that our dreams are important parts of who we are. He also has a remarkable ability to use a few questions and a few jokes to learn what things we really care about and what aspirations we hold for ourselves.

He often puts that knowledge to use. One might say he empowers us—first by acknowledging our dreams out loud, and second by encouraging us to feel we can become what we aspire to be. This encouragement has helped many individuals get charitable endeavors started in Santa Barbara.

On another level, Larry also taps into our aspirational selves to help us think beyond our daily realities and see what we can do for the wider community.

At the time this book is going to press, Larry is hard at work trying to build a bridge between two very important nonprofits in Santa Barbara. Together, both serve more than 8,000 children and teenagers in our county. Once they worked together. Now, in some areas at least, organizational differences have grown to be more important than what is best for the kids.

Larry is not tackling this task by banging together the heads of rival board members. Instead, he works one on one with key members of both groups. He cajoles a little. He listens a little. He suggests a little. But mostly, he appreciates. He acknowledges the individual motivation and dreams of each player in each organization. Once they know he appreciates not only what they do but also what they want to achieve, he asks them to sign on to the dream of creating better cooperation between the two nonprofits. The goal is simple: Cooperation will help more children, more efficiently. Larry's strategy is equally straightforward: Use the common dream of helping children to inspire the adults to move beyond their differences.

The head of a different charity, the Teddy Bear Foundation, credits Larry with giving her both the encouragement and the guidance to launch the charity.

"Larry was the first person I talked to about starting the charity," says Nikki Simon. "He gave me wonderful advice. Since that day Larry has become my mentor. It is because of his kindness, generosity, patience and huge heart that the Teddy Bear Cancer Foundation is where it is today. Larry opened so many doors. He has never given up on my dream, and every time he heard a story from a family, met a child or a parent, his heart seemed to grow even more. I have no doubt that Larry has helped me become the person I am today."

Larry's Greatest Hits

"I LIKE applause, to be sure," Larry told *Santa Barbara Magazine* in 2003, "but the real payoff for me is the psychic income that comes with helping people out."

Larry talks about psychic income a lot. He defines it in different ways. It can be what a parent feels—"that rush of pride and love, the selfless feeling that even deep down you'd rather this good thing happen to your child than to yourself." It can be the emotional response he gets from his daily interactions with people—the *bonhomie* endorphins that rise in his system as he shares his *"esprit de Larry."* A third source of psychic income comes from a sense that he has made a difference to the community, that it is changed for the better.

Larry values all psychic income, but this last "community dividend" source is particularly meaningful to him. Larry does not often talk about his larger achievements in everyday conversation. He'd much rather tell a joke or a story than recite his philanthropic résumé. So I thought I'd take this opportunity to briefly outline five of Larry's top community-wide achievements.

By writing about these five, I do not wish to minimize any of the scores of other charitable projects Larry's worked on or to suggest that one nonprofit is more or less important than another. The following were chosen to suggest the range and the impact of what Larry has done.

The Santa Barbara News-Press Lifetime Achievement Awards

When contributions to the *News-Press* Christmas Fund began to plateau in the late 1980s, Larry approached then-publisher Joe Tarrer and suggested the idea of an award for supreme community service. The idea was to honor six outstanding nominees with articles in the paper, and then to have a banquet to announce the winner of the award and to raise an additional $20,000 to $30,000 for the

Christmas Fund. Larry reasoned that there were dozens of extraordinary people doing extraordinary volunteer work in the community. To have only Man and Woman of the Year Awards, did not do justice to the large group of community leaders. He felt that recognizing them was an important way to encourage others to emulate their examples. The Lifetime Achievement Award would also raise a considerable sum each year for charity. Joe Tarrer loved the idea, and over the years, it has become a *News-Press* tradition.

In 1990, with Larry no longer serving on the selection committee, his peers wasted no time in nominating him and giving him the award. A *News-Press* editorial on November 18 that year talked about Larry's contribution as a volunteer, organizer, emcee/ auctioneer and humorist. The headline read: "Larry Crandell's Jokes Unleash Many Dollars for Charities."

The Wilcox Property–Douglas Family Preserve

In 1996, a gorgeous stretch of land along the coast of Santa Barbara was saved forever for all people to use as a park. The land, originally called the Wilcox Property and now known as the Douglas Family Preserve, was not only beautiful, it was a great recreational opportunity. The entire 70-acre property was within easy reach of all city residents. A group of Santa Barbarans, together with the California Land Trust, raised $3 million to buy the land and save it from development. Actor Michael Douglas and his family contributed $600,000 to complete the fund-raising effort. Larry was part of the organizing committee that made it happen—an achievement of which he's justifiably proud.

But there's another reason that Larry's role in this project belongs among the top five. Larry himself explains it better than anyone. In a tribute to Pierre Claeyssens after the philanthropist's death in 2003, Larry said this:

"A few years ago, hundreds of volunteers gathered for the dedication of the Douglas Family Preserve, and Pierre was there. He leaned over and asked me how much more was needed to really go 'over the top.' I replied that the figure was $33,000 [to help establish an endowment to ensure that the park would be properly cared for in the future]. Then he whispered, 'If you folks raise the thirty-three thousand, I'll add a gift of $250,000.' I bolted for the microphone, interrupted the startled master of ceremonies, and blurted out the great news. The 400 or so in attendance exploded with cheers and applause, as I knew they would. Most had worked very hard on the campaign; few had given more than $100. As I returned to my seat, Pierre said in a loud whisper, 'I didn't want you to announce it!' After I reminded him of the joy he brought to the group (not to mention the financial stability he was giving to the ongoing running of the park), he resumed his normal sunny, pleasant demeanor. The next day, Pierre called to ask me the name of the payee, as he was writing the check. I told him 'Bolivia Airlines.' Then I gave him the correct name. Two days later the check arrived. The next time we met, I asked Pierre what had made him decide to add such a large amount to the several hundred thousand he had already given to the project. He replied, 'When the children of the third grade from Monroe Elementary School sang, I wanted to ensure that 60 or 70 years from now, they and others would still be able to enjoy this beautiful park.'"

For Larry, it was the perfect ending to a perfect community project. A perfect end, too, for everyone who likes nature, a walk along the coast, and the chance to enjoy them near the city.

Friends of Westmont College and the Westmont Medal

Westmont College is a small Christian college in the foothills of Montecito. On May 6, 1995, Larry, though not a Christian himself, was given the first Westmont Medal.

The following remarks come from a speech delivered on that day by the then-President of Westmont, David Winter.

> By his example, Larry Crandell demonstrates the importance of service, compassion, responsibility, discipline and generosity to Santa Barbara and to the Westmont community. His life embodies our belief that education extends beyond the classroom to include the way we conduct ourselves in the world.
>
> A prominent businessman, Larry has dedicated his life to the nonprofit sector. Serving as master of ceremonies for as many as 100 charitable events a year, he derives great joy from giving of his time and energy to people in need and to organizations developed to meet

those needs.... Perhaps the most active participant in community life that Santa Barbara has ever known, Larry has championed the cause of education and taken special interest in Westmont College. He ignited the vision of three others to join him in founding the Friends of Westmont, a group of some 2000 important community members who now support the College in a variety of ways. Always willing to give of his time, Larry has shown conviction and strength of character in addressing issues of vital importance to Westmont College.

In fact, the organization he helped found, the Friends of Westmont, played a big role in getting new, affordable housing built to accommodate the Westmont faculty.

In receiving the award, Larry characteristically made a series of jokes. But he also said he had been inspired to help Westmont "because to me Westmont represents hope."

The Montecito Family YMCA and Montecito Union School

Larry has made it clear to me that he feels uncomfortable calling this one of his great achievements. (What does he know? Remember, I work alone.) However, he does admit the undertaking—completed over a span of more than 40 years—is utterly unique in his experience.

"To have been part of such a felicitous and highly unlikely turn of events makes it one of the most memorable charity projects for me, and in terms of the Montecito community, one of the most memorable and most wonderful."

In 1960, when Larry and Marcy and their young family moved to Santa Barbara, the Montecito Family YMCA consisted of an "ordinary 1920s house" with a back yard, according to Larry. Situated on the corner of San Ysidro Road and East Valley Road, the converted house was "totally inadequate." So the YMCA board, of which Larry was a member, decided to build a new facility. Nearby, the Montecito Union School, which is on the west side of San Ysidro Road, owned a couple of acres on the east side, off Santa Rosa Lane. At the time, they could not use the land because there was a law against putting part of the school on the other side of a busy street.

The YMCA board decided to try to lease the school's unused land. "Most of the inquiry and the negotiations were done by a marvelous fellow by the name of Jim Garvin," says Larry. "We made a proposal to the school board, which was headed by a bright developer named Michael Towbes. They came up with what turned out to be a wonderful deal for the community. They leased the two acres to the YMCA at a cost of $100 a year." The term of the lease was 50 years.

The new YMCA was built in 1965 and it still stands today serving 4,500 members. For decades, it has been widely used by the community. The Montecito Union School District says in recent years more than 60 percent of its elementary school students have gone to the YMCA every week for sports and other activities. The fortuitous location has helped nurture a symbiotic public school-YMCA relationship which is without equal in our area.

Skip ahead several decades, and with years left on the lease dwindling, the Montecito YMCA thought it should make sure it could continue to function where it was. Unfortunately, there were problems. For various reasons, an extension of the lease was not possible.

In 2005, along with a number of other community supporters, Larry joined the effort to help the YMCA secure its future. The goal—raising more than $4 million.

Larry says a developer named Brian Kelly was the hero. First, he and his wife Patricia personally secured a large property next to the school. The idea was that if sufficient funds were raised, the property could be traded for the land under the YMCA. The end result would be a win/win deal: the YMCA would end up owning the land it had used for 40 years, and Montecito Union would get more than three acres of additional land contiguous to its existing grounds.

In 2006, another philanthropist, who chose anonymity, helped complete the goal. A neighbor of the school, he donated $2.7 million dollars to complete the fund-raising effort. The land swap was on. The Montecito YMCA could plan confidently for the future.

Larry lauds Brian Kelly as the architect of the deal, just as he praises Garvin and Towbes for the first deal. But Larry's role was not insignificant. He had contributed to both community efforts—four decades apart. When he was 43, the YMCA was built. When he was 83, its future was guaranteed. In between, thousands upon thousands of children and families have benefited.

The 90-Plus Party

On February 21, 2006, everyone over the age of 90 in the Santa Barbara area was invited to a special luncheon in their honor at the Doubletree Hotel. More than 250 people in the 90-plus category attended, including three over the age of 100. They had a great time, and it wouldn't have happened without Larry Crandell.

The Santa Barbara City Department of Parks and Recreation has hosted this free event since 1985. Due to budget problems, however, the event wasn't going to be held in 2006. Then Larry found out. Larry had helped put on the event for a number of years and was very fond of it. He decided he simply wouldn't let it die. In a few weeks, he raised $13,000 so that the 90-Plus Party could go ahead.

There was a band of white-haired musicians, and, as you might expect, Larry was emcee, leading sing-alongs to old favorites like "If You Knew Susie" and "When You're Smiling." He also went into the audience with his remote mike and did interviews. They were priceless. (I had the good fortune to be there.)

> *Larry:* How long have you been married?
> *90-Plus gentleman:* Forty-four years. But that's just my first
>   marriage. I've been married to my present wife for 33 years.
> *Larry:* How's it going?
> *90-Plus gentleman:* Fine. We're just getting to be on a first-name
>   basis.

Larry enjoyed the day every bit as much the 90-Plus club members. A few wags suggested he was happy because he'd finally found a party where nearly everyone else in attendance was older than him. But Larry told the *News-Press:* "The event is a labor of love. I emcee about 50 events a year now and this is one of my favorites. This particular audience really looks forward to this luncheon, much more than other audiences. So the spirit is great, the people are very responsive, and there's a lot of love in the room."

On March 29, 2006, about a month after the 90-Plus Party—the City of Santa Barbara honored Larry for his community work by naming a large room after him in a newly renovated downtown senior recreation center. Larry was invited to speak and, at the age of 82, he did something I hadn't seen him do before. He invented a tradition and wrapped it up in a joke. He pointed to a plaque on the wall that read LARRY CRANDELL ROOM and told the packed audience, "If you touch the sign before you leave, you will have good luck within two weeks." Then he added, "If you don't have good luck, please call the recreation department staff and complain to them."

Five of Larry's greatest hits. I'm sure Larry could compile another list of completely different achievements. It might include his more than 30 community awards, his official appointment as town crier for the city of Santa Barbara or his selection as a "Local Hero" by the *Santa Barbara Independent* in 1994. But any way one looks at Larry's philanthropic career, his impact on the community has been significant and lasting.

I'll leave the last word to the *News-Press* and the editorial it ran explaining why Larry, already having been honored with Santa Barbara's Man of the Year and Volunteer of the Year awards, was selected to receive the 1990 Lifetime Achievement Award.

> There is a lot more to Larry Crandell than his stage presence.... He spends many daytime hours toiling behind the scenes for dozens of organizations: the United Way, the YMCA, the Heart Association, the Easter Seal Society, the Civic Light Opera, Direct Relief International, the Council of Christmas Cheer...the list goes on and on.
>
> Larry has often said his efforts bring him "psychic income." Thankfully, his psychic income translates into the real thing for hundreds of good causes and needy people around the county.

When Arianna Was a Republican

IN THE 1990s, when Arianna Huffington, then a well-known Republican, and Kay Theimer, a well-known Democrat, were in town, Larry helped them and several community leaders put together a nonpartisan, nonprofit organization called The Partnership for the Children of Santa Barbara County. Everyone involved was concerned about the condition of children in the county. We wanted to demonstrate how people of different political persuasions could strongly disagree as to the best approach to deal with poverty and related children's issues at the national and state levels, while locally they could put aside their differences and work cooperatively on behalf of the children. The goals were to increase awareness, be an advocate for children regardless of political persuasion and raise about $1,000,000 (which the group did!) to distribute to nonprofits working on children's issues at the time.

As one can imagine, it was a fast-paced group resulting in early morning meetings that were marked by intense and passionate debate. Often at the stormiest moments, Larry would interject his spontaneous humor. It would break the tension and bring everyone back to earth. It is not an overstatement to say that Larry's humor was the glue that helped keep the group together, and his ideas provided the framework for many of the Partnership's successful fund-raising projects.

Humor coupled with caring, ideas and hard work—that describes Larry working behind the scenes to help launch this daring, but volatile project, and to make it effective.

—Bill Cirone
County Superintendent of Santa Barbara Schools

When a Statue Is Built for You

One of the successful fund-raisers for the Partnership for Children, inspired by Larry, was an opulent banquet at the home of Arianna and Michael Huffington. The occasion? Larry's 70th birthday.

Larry's friend Joe Howell was there. Joe says there is a cottage industry in charity tributes to Larry in Santa Barbara—and he himself has attended seven. Joe describes the evening at the Huffingtons' as both historic and unforgettable. It was historic in that it set a record with its conspicuously high admission charge—$1,000 a couple in 1993. With 100 people attending, that's $50,000 before a single item was auctioned. According to Larry, the total raised at the event was $235,000.

The night was unforgettable for other reasons, as Joe explains:

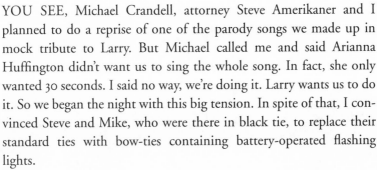

YOU SEE, Michael Crandell, attorney Steve Amerikaner and I planned to do a reprise of one of the parody songs we made up in mock tribute to Larry. But Michael called me and said Arianna Huffington didn't want us to sing the whole song. In fact, she only wanted 30 seconds. I said no way, we're doing it. Larry wants us to do it. So we began the night with this big tension. In spite of that, I convinced Steve and Mike, who were there in black tie, to replace their standard ties with bow-ties containing battery-operated flashing lights.

We got up to sing in front of 100 people. I was wearing my contacts, but something happened to them and I found I couldn't see. We began to sing anyway. The acoustics were terrible. Actually, the whole night was just off. It was a Larry nightmare—when the acoustics don't work. We had to play loud enough so the people in the back of the room could hear, but that meant we were blowing people out close to us. Michael Towbes was only about a meter away and his face was right at the guitar level. He was wincing because it was so loud and we were so pathetic. It was the single most embarrassing presentation I have ever made—terrible!

When we finished, we went into the kitchen and we were feeling incredibly embarrassed. We were so embarrassed that we didn't want to go back in and sit at our tables.

Enter Larry. The guest of honor.

He walked in calmly and said "Guys, guys, guys. I just thought about this." Then he gave us a big smile. "There's a positive in everything.—Steve, I think everybody's going to forget that you were at County Bank when it went under—because this was worse."

—Joe Howell
Howell, Moore & Gough

P.S. What made the incident funnier was that Larry had been a board member of County Bank when it experienced its misfortunes. So, in typical style, Larry was making fun of himself even as he teased a friend.

P.P.S. In its review of the event, the *News-Press* was kind to the parody singers, writing only that the "trio composed and sang several ditties about the senior Crandell's foibles."

P.P.P.S. Unfortunately, or fortunately as the case may be, the words to the trio's lead song that night ("L-L-A-R-R-Y" sung to Van Morrison's "G-L-O-R-I-A") have been lost to posterity. However, I have uncovered a similar parody penned by the same three. I include a few stanzas here.

Larry, Larry
(sung to the tune "Daisy, Daisy")

Larry, Larry, give us your answer true
You can't wait till a statue is built of you
You've had all the other honors
By now they're mostly yawners
Applause and song, won't last as long
As a statue that's built for you.

Larry, Larry, where would you like it placed?
Dolphin fountain—replaced by your smiling face?
A copper and bronze memorial
(The birds would sure enjoy y'all!)
'Twould be complete, with size twelve feet
If a statue were built for you.

Larry, Larry, how should we write the plaque?
Mister S.B.—a Santa without a sack?
When bystanders sip their coffee
They'll know you're not Kaddafi
Or Daniel Boone, or Peter Noone
When a statue is built for you.

Honor Thy Donor

ONE OF Larry's most potent fund-raising secrets is a technique that's now used by many charities. But a few decades ago that wasn't the case in Santa Barbara.

"Honoring someone was done infrequently," says Larry, "until I realized some years ago that if you honor somebody who's affluent or has affluent friends, you can raise money easily.

"Now there is Crandell's law: When in doubt, honor someone."

Larry has put the concept into practice numerous times. In the 1990s, he worked with the United Way in Santa Barbara to create an annual fund-raiser that became the Red Feather Ball. The key to making it work, says Larry, was the recruitment of philanthropists Stewart and Katherine Abercrombie—after whom the annual Abercrombie Community Excellence Awards were named.

Larry also helped the Santa Barbara Neighborhood Clinics gain public profile and raise $50,000 by developing an event that honored distinguished people and organizations in the community. "The clinics are unappreciated, unglamorous places," says Larry, "where medical and dental care is delivered to the uninsured and the underserved." With four clinics in the Santa Barbara area, the charity serves more Medi-Cal patients than anyone else in the area. "They asked if I could help with a fund-raising idea. And there are two things I like—honoring people and alliteration. So I came up with the title of Health Care Heroes, and we chose to honor a practicing medical person and a company or an individual who was helpful in fund-raising or research."

Health Care Heroes is still going strong. In 2005, the event raised $78,000.

But Larry is quick to point out that honoring a prominent individual is only a method. Nothing can substitute for a good cause. And even a good cause can struggle unless it has a good project to spur its fund-raising. One of the most effective projects is also one of the easiest to understand. In the words of the master, "Buildings are the best way to raise money."

Many nonprofits are service-oriented and need program funds above all else so they can continue to provide their philanthropic services. Many nonprofits can operate very happily in rented premises. So you might conclude that the donations easiest to garner would be for a nonprofit's services.

Wrong. Bricks and mortar win every time. Giving is not a rational exercise, and nonprofits must work in a world where emotional and personal reasons often rule.

So perhaps the most potent combination for fund-raising is a capital campaign that is supported by affluent community leaders and that honors some of those leaders.

The University of California at Santa Barbara dwarfs all other nonprofit groups in fund-raising in our area—in part because big gifts at UCSB often build edifices and create departments that honor some influential individual. Cottage Hospital's $100-million capital campaign—to replace the hospital buildings in accordance to state seismic standards—has also seen great success. Of course, UCSB and Cottage Hospital are extremely important institutions in Santa Barbara. Of course, both are deserving of the support they receive. But the ability to honor someone by building an edifice has helped their fund-raising significantly.

Of course, any rule has its exception—even a Mr. Santa Barbara rule. Buildings *are* motivating, and honoring a person of standing *is* a good idea, but celebrity can sometimes trump anything. Oprah Winfrey's successful work for Girls, Inc. in Santa Barbara is one example. Another is the story of Larry and the Dalai Lama.

Larry was raising money for the Santa Barbara-based and internationally known charity Direct Relief International (DRI) in the 1990s. DRI works hard to reduce the costs of its philanthropy by delivering donated medical supplies directly to hospitals and medical clinics in need. It has a reputation for quality service and for actively seeking donations to extend its reach. On this particular afternoon, Stewart and Katherine Abercrombie were hosting a small gathering at their Montecito home. Twenty five people had been invited.

Larry greeted the guests as they came in—including the Dalai

Lama himself. Then he thought he saw a familiar face. A very hand-some man with gray hair. It was Richard Gere, a follower of the Tibetan spiritual leader. As Larry greeted the actor, Stewart Aber-crombie wandered by. "You're someone famous," said Stewart. "What's your name?" Larry quickly introduced the host to his famous guest.

They all went inside. And there, something remarkable happened. Larry, who spends most of his time introducing well-known people, was himself introduced by one of the most famous people on the planet.

The Dalai Lama, with a friendly smile on his face, said simply. "I want you to listen to Mr. Crandell."

It was the closest Larry ever came to spiritual enlightenment. Liter-ally. Larry was only about five feet away from the Tibetan leader.

Larry then turned to his task, raising money from the well-heeled group. But before he could get out much more than the intended goal of raising $25,000, someone spoke up. He offered five thousand dol-lars.

Before Larry could reply, someone else said, "Let's just take Larry out of his misery. I'll put up 10 grand if someone else will." Someone else did, and that was that.

Three donors in as many minutes. Total to DRI: $25,000.

Larry suspects the speed of the process might have had something to do with the fact that he was on first and the people there that day were slightly more interested in what the Dalai Lama had to say. In any case, the fund-raising was as easy as it gets.

Take a Chance with Your Conversation

HERB SIMON, co-owner of the Indiana Pacers and owner of the biggest shopping center in Minneapolis, lives in Santa Barbara. In 2000, one of his children was attending the private Waldorf school in Santa Barbara. Larry was doing an auction for the school, and he called Herb to make sure he would be there. It was a logical assumption because the auction was to be held at Herb's Montecito home. But the NBA owner had an impressive excuse. "Larry," he said, "it's the fifth game of the NBA finals." The Pacers were vying for the championship against the Lakers. Larry naturally understood why Herb would be unable to attend, but the auctioneer in him didn't want to give up. "That's no problem, Herb," Larry said. "Just send one of your people with ten thousand dollars to bid." It might have come over as a terribly crass thing to say, except that Larry's cheeky, ironic delivery made it feel like part of the normal banter the two men shared. On the day of the auction (and the fifth game), Herb did generously delegate someone to bid for him—and the delegate spent exactly $10,000. The Waldorf School was the winner on the day. Unfortunately, the Pacers lost the fifth game and the series.

Larry's greatest fund-raising weapon is himself. There is no one like him. He combines compassion with perception, a deep skepticism about "good intentions" with a deep belief in "good acts," a cool rationality with an almost sentimental reaction to want and suffering. Then he ties it all together with an insouciant, mischievous sense of humor and a consummate ability to communicate.

Larry's communication strategy is based on the element of surprise.

One of the biggest fans of the Larry approach to conversation is a man named Demetri E. Argyropoulous, president and CEO of Prima Consulting. He first met Larry when he was 14.

"I call Larry my illegitimate grandfather, " said Demetri. "I come from a Greek family, and my real grandfather was my closest friend. He died when I was 19. Since then, I've seen Larry at least a half-dozen times a year. He's my mentor. Larry taught me how to communicate. He says things to people to shock them, but always in a joking way. It breaks the ice and creates an atmosphere of intimacy, trust and vulnerability. It's a great atmosphere for fund-raising."

"I take more chances conversationally than almost everybody," Larry said to reporter Ben Hellwarth in a 1993 *News-Press* article. "But I find it's a good way to clasp hands or create a bond. I enjoy taking chances. The downside is embarrassment, but I end up with a lot of very good acquaintances."

Larry lives for the repartee when, as Hellwarth put it, "someone matches him wisecrack for wisecrack." And Larry hates the most used conversational device in America—the simple question, how are you? "People don't mean it most of the time. And they aren't really interested in the answer. I'd rather go up to a guy and say—'I'm really disappointed to see you. (Pause) I thought I was going to be the best-looking guy in the restaurant.' Or approach an older couple and say, "Now, that's wonderful. How many men would take their *daughter* out for lunch?"

The response is often laughter and a sense of shared fun—for Larry, the opposite of meaningless conversational ritual.

"Other people do exactly what I do and call it schmoozing," Larry said in the same 1993 article. "But to me, to 'schmooze' somebody is to have a motive other than a desire to please them, to communicate friendliness and warmth, to value them. It's okay to call others schmoozers. I think I should be called charming. It's all very logical."

There's another reason why Larry wouldn't do very well as a true schmoozer or sycophant. While he's often noted for being self-deprecating, he's also quite good at deprecating others. He always does it in a good-natured way, but the end result is far from flattery and often finishes where Larry begins life—in an ironic tone.

Reporter Hellwarth writes:

> At a Channel City Club luncheon, just as Crandell, the president, took center stage and greeted the audience, someone shot back: "Hi, Larry."

Without missing a beat, Crandell looked over, flipped through his mental archive, and then said, "Yale, Class of '29, right?"

"You got it!" the silver-haired man said jubilantly.

"Have they made that a four-year school yet?" Crandell asked.

A Prelude to Faith

LARRY'S marvel and magic is that he makes it all about me, not about himself. Even when the topic is Larry—to whom he frequently alludes—it's simply a way of making me feel at ease, welcome, wanted, admired, important and needed. He verbally embraces us with hugful and humorous insight. He always makes me think of Reinhold Niebuhr's statement:

"Humor is a prelude to faith, and laughter is the beginning of prayer."

Larry helps us to be holy. I once wrote of him that he deflates our pomposity and dares us to be real, to care more for one another and to have fun doing all these things. His observations are wise, his lessons are gentle. His wry but compassionate acceptance of the human condition makes us all feel better about ourselves and each other and encourages us to strive to live up to his funny, funny view of us.

—Maryellen Kelley
Director, Omega Program,
Adult Education, Santa Barbara City College

Everything's Connected to Humor

"I ride a stationary bicycle for 45 minutes daily. When I finish I'm exactly where I started. It's a metaphor for my life."

—*Mr. Santa Barbara, quoted in the* News-Press, *2003*

LARRY approaches a small group of people in the minutes before a charity event starts. He has no microphone, no podium, no stage, and yet MC Larry is already in full performance mode.

"Do you know Rene Descartes?" Larry says.

"Yes," says a woman. There is a nod or two. But the group is tentative. They are aware that in such a situation, Larry is usually doing one of two things—setting up a humorous trap or springing it.

Larry smiles. "Rene's the one who said, 'I think, therefore I am.'"

The listeners relax a bit. They all nod now.

"Well, I was only a kid when he was writing his great treatise, but since then I've revised his philosophy."

He leans forward slightly, lowering his voice. "When you're over 80, it's 'I ache, therefore I am.'"

The gray-haired listeners smile. Some laugh. There is both pleasure and understanding. Larry, lord of levity, is in command, and all is right with the world.

Humor is both a means and an end for Larry—the trusty steed on which he gallops and the Holy Grail he seeks. He once gave a speech with the subject "What Matters Most." Larry's position was unequivocal: humor. In this sense, he is hardly any different whether he's at the mike or across the table at a café. Laughter and wordplay provide manna for him at any time. His ability to cope with life's difficulties, his ease in connecting with people, his effectiveness at communication and fund-raising, his community leadership—all these attributes depend on his being funny. When he says that for him everything is connected to humor, he is being very serious.

As he begins to talk about his theory of humor, one can see some of his trademarks in relief—the short, ironic anecdote, the free-ranging narrative that layers stories to build an effect, the asides that show he doesn't take himself too seriously (so the audience can relax and have some fun), the odd philosophical observation and the driving force of all his conversation, sheer entertainment.

Larry's muse often works best when he uses his humanness as the source of his humor. Part of the delight of listening to Larry is that he honestly refers to his clay feet even as he dances gracefully.

I'll let you listen to what I'm talking about. This is Larry talking to me on tape in 2006 about being funny.

∽

I think humor can be a lubricant. It can be a simple thing. When I go to open the door for people at the Coral Casino Beach and Cabana Club, where there are no indigent members, I say, "No tipping, please."

Or someone opens it for me and I say, "Sorry, I don't tip." Which for some reason is only half as funny. It would be interesting to study that. I have a keen interest in the unimportant. It's kind of my specialty. Who else would want to ponder why when you're the potential tipper it's less funny than when you're the potential tippee?

Humor is also a wonderful way to indicate affection, especially with men. For example, a local philanthropist bids at an auction to rescue me (because no one else is bidding). And I say, "By the way folks, there's a hero here. Over the years, he's bid over one million dollars at charity auctions—and never bought anything."

Or I'll start a lunch meeting by saying a guy is a buck short on his lunch money—even though everyone knows he's a multi-millionaire. Then I'll go on in mock seriousness, saying, "Well, there are several ways we can raise the dough. Nine cents a month for 12 months would do it. But of course, if someone would pledge it all at once that would be easier."

One man got a verbal kiss from me every time I saw him at an auction. His name was Paul Ridley-Tree—he was kind, gentle. He and his wife, Leslie, gave away tens of millions of dollars to Santa Barbara charities. At one auction, he was the only bidder, and out of pure pity for me, he raised his own bid. So every time he bid at an auction after that, I told the story.

I've been accused of digression. I get criticized for getting off the subject. What I'm trying to do is orchestrate a mood.

For instance, at the Channel City Club. Did you notice the relative antiquity? I get up to the mike and sigh, "I want to tell a story. Is there anyone in the room who remembers World War Two?" Or, "How many of you were in the service? [pause] How many of you were on our side?" Why is that funny? I don't know, but people laugh.

❧

Laughter has been a natural part of Larry's life since childhood. Larry remembers his mother's comic inspiration despite the hard times of the Depression.

"Even then humor was so much a part of it," Larry told the *News-Press* in 1993. "My mother would walk in—I can just picture her then with bundles of groceries—she had to take two buses to get home. Of course, we had no car. And the instant she opened the door, the three of us boys would yell: "Is dinner ready yet?"

"But you know, how can you do dinner if you just finished climbing the stairs? And she was almost always very, very cheerful, very upbeat, a very count-your-blessings type. She would laugh and say, 'Not yet, boys. Be ready soon!'"

The same newspaper article recounted Larry's story of how humor helped him cope with difficult times.

> Larry recalled visiting his brother in a New York hospital. The bedside scene seemed strangely reminiscent of the final moments in the 1970 film *Love Story*, which Crandell said is "one of the half-dozen movies that are most memorable to me."
>
> "Marty, my brother, was out of it. So I leaned over and whispered in his ear: 'Move over, Marty. I'm going to crawl in with you the way Ryan O'Neal did with Ali MacGraw,'" Crandell recalled.
>
> "When he came out of it about two months later, he

said: 'I could have killed you. I couldn't move or talk, and I thought I was going to blow all these tubes out. And my clown of a brother is acting up at what should be a very serious time.'"

The incident remains, Crandell said, "a delicious memory."

"I thought, here are two guys who weigh about 450 pounds [together], about to crawl into bed with one another. It struck me as funny, and struck *him* as funny. But that was one of the ways we said, 'I love you.'"

Though Larry loves to say something totally unexpected to get a laugh, he doesn't like to surprise people by introducing humor when they don't expect it. "I try to be transparent with myself and my humor," he says. "My rule is, if I smile, I'm saying to people, 'Watch out.'"

Larry's comic palette is only as limited as his imagination, but many of his sallies of fun fall into one of several categories.

"First of all there's shock value. People like to be surprised. They like to see prominent people taken down a peg. There's a certain accountant in town. Very successful. His employees would like to put him on a rotisserie, so they revel in my freedom in teasing him.

"There's also hyperbole. You know, the mother saying to the son, 'I've told you a thousand times, don't exaggerate.' Hyperbole can also bring home reality. For instance, the recent introduction of hearing aids enhanced my life, but it also had some unintended consequences. The toilet flushing now sounds like Niagara Falls. And the turn signal on my car sounds like a train crossing."

Larry's silver tongue is sharp. But as often as Larry teases people—he calls himself "an equal opportunity insulter"—he says it's never a case of one-upmanship.

"I do have a little philosophy, and that is to let the audience know that I don't take myself seriously. Sometimes with groups I know well I'll say something that is outlandishly braggart. For example, I hold my hand over the heads of myself and another person to decide which emcee is better. The applause is unanimous for the other guy. But I always say, 'Well, it's close, but I won.' That gets hoots. I find audiences are grateful if you clearly show that you don't take yourself too seriously and that you're going to try to amuse them. People decide fairly quickly who you are."

Larry clowns for good causes and often tells jokes for high stakes—raising money for life-saving, family-supporting charities. But he is not a proselytizer or even a salesman for their causes. He never brow-beats audiences or donors. Instead, he treats them like friends—friends he wants to show a very good time.

Larry's approach to humor means taking risks. Jokes can bomb. Audiences can be tough. Auctions can fail to fire. But it's all part of the deal. "To be a chance taker in the spotlight and to be very vulnerable makes for a never-dull existence. And when it works, it's thrilling. Thrilling, to be well-received. When I'm letting the applause and laughter die down, that's food and drink. Sustenance. I get goose pimples just thinking about it. It's a non-drug high."

Keep the Material, Change the Audience

"HAVE I told you this story?"

This is one of the most used questions in Larry's verbal arsenal. And it has nothing to do with short-term memory loss. He asks it for two reasons:

1. He loves recycling stories and jokes.
2. He doesn't want to get caught doing it.

"This will shock you, my son," he's told me, with a dead earnest look on his face. "But if the situation's different, I have no conscience about using the same material. Give me a hundred different situations and I can be original without thinking of a single new thing."

When Larry and Marcy were Grand Marshalls of the Santa Barbara Fourth of July parade down State Street, he felt very proud. There were marching bands and floats. People rode well-groomed horses. Red, white and blue bunting was draped on everything stationary and most things that moved. In the midst of it all, Mr. and Mrs. Santa Barbara rode in the back seat of a large convertible— taking pride of place.

It was great, but Larry wanted to add his own touch to the patriotic occasion. When the parade paused every 100 yards or so, Larry would stand in the car and shout out, *"¡Viva la Fiesta!"* All the children lining the parade route would hasten to correct him, informing him that this was our nation's birthday, not Santa Barbara's Old Spanish Days.

Larry would act the fool and trade wisecracks and jokes with the onlookers until the parade started to move again. As soon as the procession had advanced to a new group of people, Larry would stand and shout out, *"¡Viva la Fiesta!"* The new group of children would immediately chide him for his "mistake," and the fun would start again.

Three words in Spanish, expertly misplaced, got him big reaction after big reaction. Larry loved it. And as the parade never covered the same ground twice, repetition held no risk. It is perhaps the most striking example of how a new audience can make all the difference.

"There are no old jokes, only old audiences," says Larry, appropriately quoting an old saying. "I don't need to be a pioneer. I'm looking for results."

Larry can make this strategy work in part because he can cope when it fails. He is so good at ad-libbing that he can create humor from the fact that he has been caught repeating a story. In fact, stories about his own foibles and mistakes fit right in with his "I don't take myself seriously" persona.

You see, Larry takes pride in his humility. As he once said to an admirer, "I don't think I'm half as good as I really am."

A Tango with the Conscience

LARRY Crandell represents the conscience of our community. With humor and bite, he points out our pretentiousness and leads us towards being more giving and loving. The only reason I'll go to some fancy fund-raising event is to enjoy seeing maestro Crandell pick apart the Montecito set. I believe he shares genes with Groucho Marx.

There is an incident that sums up the zany wit, elegance and charm of our ambassador of common humanity. It was brought to mind by a photograph depicting Larry and my then 18-year-old daughter, Gena, dancing together. I had found it on the kitchen table upon arriving home one night. Using Larry's style of humor, I indignantly asked her, "What were you doing with that rascal?" The following is Gena's description:

"Dancing a tango through the purse department of Saks Fifth Avenue isn't exactly an everyday occurrence, at least without the presence of Larry Crandell. He had arrived, dressed in a lustrous gray suit, to help promote the Profant Foundation's silent auction, and I was the poster girl for the event. The buzz of Fiesta was in the air, and I donned a full flamenco outfit to match the theme. Larry made his way from the entrance to where I stood. Without much of an introduction, he grabbed my waist with one arm and took my hand in his. He furrowed his brow and led me in an impressive bit of choreography among the glass display cases.

"I later found out he was 80 years old at the time of our tango."

—Andy and Gena Davis
Film director/producer (Holes, The Guardian)
and Tufts University Student

He Just Has Fun All Day

I found this revealing anecdote in a program for a Transition House bene-
fit event. Transition House helps Santa Barbara families cope with home-
lessness, offering shelter, food and services with the goal of getting these
families back into permanent housing. One of Larry's favorite charities,
Transition House put together a tribute to him to raise money in 1997.

   Rita Murdoch offered this story for the event—it's about the day her
daughter Christine spent with Larry "at work."

❧

CHRISTINE had a school assignment in seventh grade—around
Career Day—to go to work with her father. Her father lives in L.A.,
but Larry graciously volunteered to stand in. Christine accompanied
him, starting early, to an appointment with Peter MacDougall, then
president of Santa Barbara City College; they visited Hal Conklin,
then mayor of Santa Barbara; they went on to see Steven Ainsley, then
publisher of the *News-Press*; soon afterwards, they lunched with yet
another Santa Barbara dignitary. When Christine wrote her report on
this day in the work world, one of the questions she was required to
answer was: "What does he do?" She quickly filled in that line by
writing—"He just has fun all day."

—*Rita Murdoch*
Christine's mother

The Dis-invitation

IT'S DISARMING. It's distinctive. It's disingenuous.

Apologies to Cole Porter, but one of Larry's most subtle ploys is all about wordplay. He calls the conversational strategy a "dis-invitation." On the surface, it seems straightforward: Larry dis-invites people to nonprofit fund-raisers—outwardly excusing them from attending, while at the same time informing them of the event. He also manages to inform them of *his* participation in the event—usually as the emcee or auctioneer.

The dis-invitation is never disrespectful. It's a ruse that's meant to be seen as a ruse. Larry looks magnanimous while doing subtle marketing for charity. The dis-invitee is let off the hook gently. There is a sense of relief when the listener finds the Silver Tongue doesn't actually expect anything. What could be more polite than to *not* attend a fund-raiser to which you were dis-invited?

And if someone really does want to come to the event in question, a dis-invitation can be quickly transformed to an invitation.

This particular Silver Tongue secret opens the door to humor—Larry loves to explain why the dis-invitee will never regret staying away from this particular function. It also builds Larry's relationship and his history with you. Once you've been dis-invited, you feel the slightest bit beholden to support Larry in some way. After all, he *has* been gracious in excusing you.

Larry will not seek to use this advantage immediately. Instead, he'll save it. When the time is right, Larry will appear again—except this time he will be bearing an *in*vitation, and he'll be asking for your help.

Larry the Yenta

PEOPLE laud Larry for his service to the community, and many of his efforts are quite public. But he also loves to help people in quiet, personal ways. Sometimes, this help is fairly straightforward networking—Larry using his Rolodex to help someone find a job or a volunteer or a board member or a donor. Sometimes, he shows his flair, sending roses to people who have hit hard times with the note—"These are not from whom you expect." As with the Brad Pitt stratagem, most people guess it's Larry straight away. Still, the ploy usually inspires smiles where there were frowns, and the recipients invariably appreciate Larry's silly secrecy.

His favorite behind-the-scenes role, however, is as a matchmaker. Larry says he'd love to start his own *pro bono* dating service because he gets such a kick out of getting people together.

About 10 years ago, he experienced perhaps his greatest success.

The woman, we'll call her Daphne, was a warm, vivacious psychotherapist in her forties. She had experienced tragedy a few years prior: her fiancé had died in a traffic accident, and since then, she had not found love.

The man, we'll call him Ed, was a business executive. Larry describes him as a "Dick Tracy type" with silver hair. He was divorced—and it hadn't been amicable. At one point, his ex-wife had told him he was "the dullest male human being in the world." And to be truthful, he wasn't especially sparkly. But he had a good heart.

Ed told Larry he was tired of dating and wanted to meet a "nice lady" for a long-term relationship. So Larry asked Daphne if she would go out with Ed. She accepted and the pair went out for dinner. Larry didn't hear anything for two weeks. Then Daphne called Larry and said she had two tickets to the symphony and asked Larry to ask Ed if he would accompany her. Larry was thrilled to have his Cupid capabilities called on once again. But when he talked to Ed, every-thing unraveled.

"I have someone coming to visit that weekend," Ed said, and by that he meant he had arranged to see another woman. Larry immedi-ately called Daphne and told her the news, thinking that the truth straight out would be the easiest way to limit the pain. Larry thought it just wasn't going to work, and having failed as a matchmaker, at least he could offer Daphne a sympathetic ear.

To his surprise, Daphne said she wanted to talk to Ed. Larry arranged the meeting and was flabbergasted at the result.

You see, Ed told Daphne that he had adored her ten minutes after he met her, but he knew he wouldn't have a chance with her. So he had given up and moved on.

This is Larry's favorite part of the story. "I've told this story 50 times," he says, "and I always ask the women I tell—'Should she have believed this guy?' Almost every woman says: absolutely not. He's a lying S.O.B. But Daphne believed him, and in fact, he was being honest."

Four months later, Ed and Daphne were married in a very small ceremony in Santa Barbara. Larry gave Daphne away. ("I recall I was wearing a blue double-breasted jacket," says Larry.) It's one of Larry's fondest memories in a life full of fond memories.

"They are deliriously happy," he says. And for years after the wed-ding, they'd send Larry a bottle of wine and flowers on their anniver-sary. Jane, the Jewish mother, would have been proud. Her own son, a *yenta*!

Concern, Support and an Open Door

I HAVE known Larry since I was 23 years old. We were both working for the Littlestone Company then. Larry was a vice president, and I worked in data entry.

I was one of two women chosen to travel around the country doing auditing for the company. Larry called me into his office, gave me an extra briefcase he had and walked me through how to conduct myself while representing the company. He treated me like a father treats a daughter—with concern, support and an open door. I knew I could count on him for any advice or direction I needed.

Then, when the company was preparing to close, I ended up in the hospital for three weeks. Larry knew I was putting my husband through UCSB and would not be able to pay my hospital bills. He went to the president of Littlestone and asked that the company cover my insurance costs until I was up and around. As a result I had 100 percent hospitalization and was able to go through my treatments with great peace of mind.

Years later, after I had left town to go to college and returned to Santa Barbara divorced, I was working for an old friend of Larry's and we reconnected. One day when I told Larry I was engaged, he said, "Who's the lucky fella?" When I told him, he said, "Oh six-four, 225 pounds, played football for USC." I couldn't believe it—he not only knows everyone, he remembers everything about them.

With Larry, I know that I have a knight in shining armor right in my pocket, even though I hate to ask him for anything, because everyone in town asks him. Larry is just the best friend anyone could ever have. He makes me laugh no matter how dire things seem and makes himself available whenever there is need. I don't want to imagine a world without him.

—*Kate Carter*
Founder and executive director, Life Chronicles, Inc.

Respect Everyone

LARRY used to entertain his children, especially me, by telling us stories of "Backwards Land"—where grown-ups have to take naps, children stay up late and you get in trouble for eating your vegetables. I used to love to talk with him about all the crazy and wonderful things that happened in Backwards Land.

But for Larry, it isn't just a diversion for children. Every day, he turns the world of status and privilege on its head, doing the opposite of what people expect him to do. Though he has achieved great standing in the community and hobnobs with the local gentry, he makes a point of not observing his proper place on the social ladder.

Here are the four main rules of interpersonal relations, according to Larry:

1. Respect everyone.
2. Be friendly whenever possible.
3. Be irreverent with the affluent and powerful.
4. Be solicitous of those who are normally ignored.

Larry often goes to fancy affairs and ends up in conversations with the waiters. Or he works out at an exclusive club and starts drawing out the janitorial staff on their personal lives. At lunch, he will meet important people and proceed to focus on their spouses or children.

Larry is classless when it comes to relating to other people. Perhaps it's because he had humble beginnings. Perhaps he simply loves to talk with people and ignores the difference in status. But in any case, he cultivates relationships with people who have neither wealth, nor power—asking about their families, their work, their studies, their dreams, their sporting preferences and sometimes even doing something special for them.

One time, Larry got to know a porter at one of the big hotels in town, one of the nicest in the whole region. When Larry found out the porter had a toothache, Larry arranged with his own dentist to give him care.

Another time, Larry stepped in to help a waiter at the Biltmore Hotel. We'll call him Diego. I'll let Larry tell the story.

◞

DIEGO was a tall good-looking man from the center of Mexico. He'd drive back every year in his Trans Am and be a hero in his remote little hometown. He smiled all the time—which was more noticeable because he had a gold tooth in the front. He was the sweetest man, and he was very much in love.

Then one day I noticed he had become unusually reserved. A few days later I saw him again, and he was really glum. When I asked him why, he told me an act of love had backfired on him. He had taken his significant other's clothes to the laundromat to wash them, but had ended up nearly destroying them.

I listened sympathetically. Then I asked Diego how much he thought it would cost to replace the clothes. He said about a hundred and fifty bucks. Now, there are smooth ways of helping someone, and there's the direct way, which sometimes shames them. I didn't know how to be smooth in this particular instance. So I said, "Diego, I'm going to do something that will offend you. And if you say anything, I'm going to call up your boss and tell him how terrible you are."

"Don't do that," he said.

"What I'm going to do is hand you a hundred-dollar bill," I explained. "I want you to know I'm getting $500 dollars worth of pleasure out of it. I want to help you get back in the good graces of your girl, because I don't know anyone who loves with the purity that you do."

He's hugged me 4,812 times since then to thank me. And I think that's just the interest.

He bought his sweetheart new clothes, and the next time I saw him he was smiling again.

Wednesdays with Larry

NOTHING can seduce Larry like a funny or clever line. When he comes up with something he feels is both funny and clever, he becomes besotted. Reason matters little. Objectivity is abandoned. Like the mythical king Pygmalion, he falls in love with his own creation.

So it was with "Wednesdays with Larry." He liked the phrase so much he decided it had to be the title of this book. We would meet every Wednesday morning at Moby Dick restaurant on Santa Barbara's Stearns Wharf—his favorite breakfast spot. We would talk. I would take notes. Then *Tuesdays with Morrie* would become yesterday's book!

You should have seen his face fall when I told him that it was a fantastic title—for a chapter. The corners of his mouth took the express elevator down, and he was frowning in seconds. "So it's not good enough," he mock-harrumphed. But the genuine *harrumph* could not be disguised. For all his verbal derring-do, Larry is really a very sensitive soul. He senses rejection as easily as he does acceptance.

But he is also resilient. And his mock *harrumph* disappeared when we began the first of our Wednesdays with Larry in August 2005.

Unfortunately, due to scheduling problems, the first Wednesday session was held on a Thursday. But the Crandell Company is nothing if not flexible.

Here are a few of my notes from that day:

> Outline was discussed. Larry emphasized that he want-
> ed to avoid pomposity. I told him that frankly I thought
> it was a bit pompous to attempt such a blanket ban. He
> said he considered "boring people was a crime very close
> to manslaughter." Which means he wants the book to

be a page-turner.... He also wants the book to have universal appeal. I told him there were certain limitations based on the subject matter.... He talked about his subversive approach to perfunctory greetings. He said, "Discussing the weather is enough to make me scream...." An 85-year-old woman walked slowly past the table, leaning heavily on a cane. Larry crowed to her, "I'll never forget last night." She beamed.

It was the first of many talks. Because our offices are only five paces apart and my questions were numerous, we ended up talking frequently. Wednesdays with Larry became Every Day with Larry. For me, it was a blessing. For him, well, he said it was a joy. He may want to revisit that assessment once he reads what I've written.

At Moby Dick, there's a table dedicated to Mister Santa Barbara. Larry calls it a shrine. But so far, I haven't spotted any graven images. Just framed photos and press clippings on the wall and a model of a B-24 bomber with bomb-bay doors open positioned directly over the chair where Larry's guests sit. This is the place you are most likely to talk with Larry when you first meet him. His breakfast order—eggs sunny-side up, toast and bacon with sliced tomato—is so well known to the waiting staff there that Larry just wiggles his fingers in the air like a magician and they write it on their pads.

Larry is at home here, and as I imagine him seated at his own shrine, talking to someone, drawing them out, spinning his own yarns, one of his favorite quotes comes to mind. It's Ralph Waldo Emerson again:

"What you do speaks so loudly, I can't hear what you say."

For Larry, words are paramount, and speaking is in fact how he fills most of his days. However, the truest description of his character can be found not so much in the content of his conversation, but in the personal relationships and actions affected by that conversation.

Who is Larry Crandell then?

Larry is someone who loves getting people to help others. He wants to reduce suffering. But he would admit in a flash that he derives the most fun from helping others enjoy life. And how does he do that? In part, by enjoying himself as he helps, by reveling in the process of enhancing someone else's position. Larry describes himself as extremely other-oriented, but he is self-directed in equal measure.

Larry once summed it up this way: "You can't help others without helping yourself."

His life is not about sacrifice. It is about fulfillment. To serve others, he needs to do some self-serving at the same time. Does that mean there needs to be something for Larry in a charity project? Yes, of course. But the remarkable number of charities and individuals he's helped over the years attest to the fact that it's easy for Larry to find that something. His enjoyment often stems simply from the sense that he has made a difference (while getting a few laughs and a number of rounds of applause.)

In this sense, Larry has found a way to care for himself and the community at the same time. He is simultaneously self-focused and altruistic. For Larry, there is a "me" in "team"—and there is no shame in recognizing it.

No surprise then, that Larry regards his work as his play. No surprise that the journey is all. No surprise that he seems indefatigable. As the girl who shadowed him on Career Day found out, he's really having fun.

Larry's life is the story of counting your blessings by making sure a few more blessings are bestowed on the people around you. I see it every day now. He says it's "easy to be Larry Crandell." But few others could ever pull it off.

Being happy and creating happiness are two different things. In my father, I have seen the capacity do both.

Love in a Pot

"If you want to please someone you love, do something nice or thoughtful or meaningful for someone they love."

There it is. In 19 words, Larry reveals one of his most potent secrets. It usually takes a moment or two, but when most people think about it, they get it. They nod. They smile. Of course. One of Larry's gifts is being pithy. Another is having insight and honesty about what it means to be human. Here, he is exploring a paradox—how you can show love to someone by directing kindness and consideration to someone else.

"The simplest way in the world to please a parent," says Larry, "is to do something nice for his or her children."

It also works in reverse. You can please the child by doing something for the parent. Larry tells a story to illustrate this principle.

∽

MY MOTHER-IN-LAW was Lena Novak. She expressed love through cooking. So I would fast the day we were going to visit her. I felt that a gift I could give Marcy would be to accept and appreciate her parents and to be regarded fondly by them. Well, Big Mike Novak, 6-foot-4, railroad engineer—was a gentle giant. Very pleasant fellow. We got on well from the beginning. Lena and I had less in common.

So Marcy and I would drive the 100 miles to their house in Ashley, Pennsylvania. It took a couple of hours. We'd come in and first thing, I'd say, "Do you have anything to eat, Lena. I'm starving."

"You just come with me," she'd say, and she'd take me into the kitchen. She was a good cook, and I wanted to recognize her milieu. It wasn't that hard. I wanted to please her. It comes from my mother. Pleasing people is very satisfying to me.

∽

Love in a pot. Grandma Lena always made enough food for seconds and thirds. We always left her table feeling full and satisfied. But Larry's point is that eating Lena's food with gusto made her *feel satisfied, too. And that, in turn, was a way to say "I love you" to Marcy.*

One might say that this process lacks directness. One might say that messages in code, even positive messages, can be misread or go unnoticed. But to me, life is inherently convoluted, relationships are naturally complicated, and love is an intricate weaving together of experience.

Love in a pot suits me fine. So does Larry's secret weapon of appreciation. "Every loving act carries with it the power to transform lives, so all kindness matters." That's one of the foundation stones of Larry's life. Mine, too.

I can see Larry smiling now—pleased that he has found a way to be pleasing. He does feel shallow things deeply, you know. But what he doesn't admit to many is that he feels deep things deeply, too.

Za-boo-la-roo!

I wrote this letter to my father for his 82nd birthday. It seems a fitting way to finish this book about Larry—with a magic word.

∽

DEAR DAD,

"Za-boo-la-roo!"

Josette shouted it from her car seat in the back of our van. A split second later, the light turned green and we were moving again.

"Wow, you're magic," I told her over my shoulder. But I was only stating the obvious. As I looked at her, I saw the delight in her eyes and the big smile. She's a clever two-year-old. She knew it was a game, but she also believed. Dad was full of jokes and tricks and stories, she knew that. But she had said Grandpa's magic word, and the light had turned green. That was magic.

Josette is at the wonderful age where she wants to suspend disbelief and does so as easily as she smiles or runs or changes her dress-up clothes. Anything is possible. So enjoyment is never beyond her—even when she'd just had an inoculation and she was feeling tired and impatient to get home, as was the case today.

Of course, you, Dad, taught me *"Za-boo-la-roo"* decades ago as we waited at lights in Santa Barbara.

I still hold the word dear. It turns tedious waiting into a game. It transforms a mundane intersection into a stage for conjuring. It bends the preordained to our will. It creates a tall tale and then makes it real.

Say it with high seriousness—but don't forget the twinkle in the eye. The four-syllable incantation—*Za-boo-la-roo!*

(I can see you doing your magic hand motion at the lights as you sit at the wheel of the recently repainted beige 1967 Impala. What a car that was!)

Za-boo-la-roo also has the very useful quality of not having its magic diminished by repetition. How many times did I try to master the trick of the timing as a child, and how many times did I end up saying the magic word a dozen or more times before "making" the lights change?

It was in the 1960s that you played the game with me. It was 2005, today in fact, that I played the game with Josette. The result was the same: fun for father and child, *joie de vivre* at the traffic lights.

Now *that* is magic.

It might interest you to know that we tried other magic words. I came up with *Abrakadabra*, and Kathleen suggested *Alakazam!* To no effect. Only *Za-boo-la-roo* did the trick.

As we rode back today, Kathleen at the wheel, I smiled at my wife and she smiled conspiratorially back at me. Then I couldn't help but steal another glance back at Josette in her car seat. The grin was still stretched across her face, the magic word still playing on her lips.

I thought of how I plagiarize all those things I love about your parenting, and how it is not just the genes that are passed down, but the method of living.

On this your 82nd birthday, I want to thank you for teaching me such a useful and powerful word. I spend a fair amount of time trying to appreciate the moments that inject joy into existence—I even like to create a few. You taught me that waiting for a red light to turn to green could be fun, could be funny, could be a memory to hold on to all my life. You taught me that enjoyment isn't something that always comes to you, it is something that can be created.

Critics say stories are told in details. So, too, are lives acted out. And when, on occasion, those details take on meaning, the ephemeral becomes something lasting, something worth remembering. Like when you're with your dad at the stoplight, saying *Za-boo-la-roo*. Or when your daughter uses the magic word for the very first time.

Thanks, Dad.

I love you.

Steven

Epilogue

IF YOU thought Larry wouldn't get the last word in his own book, think again.

He didn't want to offer advice on fund-raising, though he could have. He didn't want to talk about the state of the nonprofit world, though he has enough experience to hold an enlightened opinion. He didn't even want to tell a funny story, though he does that about as often as he exhales.

Instead, he wanted to leave you with this blessing:

> *May you make your life from a pattern*
> *Designed and re-designed by your heart.*
> *No matter how clever you are,*
> *No matter how rich,*
> *No matter, even, how funny you are,*
> *Nothing equals love.*
> *May it define your home, your journey and your destination,*
> *And may it help you appreciate and enjoy the people around you.*

> *With Love,*
> *Larry Crandell*